Vegetable Heaven

Vegetable Heaven
Catherine Mason

paintings by
Elda Abramson

Grub Street • London

Published in 2006 by
Grub Street
4 Rainham Close
London
SW11 6SS
Email: food@grubstreet.co.uk
Web: www.grubstreet.co.uk

Reprinted 2006

First published in hardback by Pauntley Press

A CIP catalogue record for this book is available from the British Library

ISBN 1 904943 53 5

Printed and bound in India

CONTENTS

COOKING NOTES AND ACKNOWLEDGMENTS

INGREDIENTS

It goes without saying that in *Vegetable Heaven* all food is produced without chemical assistance. Good husbandry and best growing practice prevail. Fruit and vegetables are grown organically, and eggs come from happy, free-range hens! Olive oil is extra virgin and cold-pressed. Pepper is usually black and always freshly ground in a mill. Salt is additive-free sea salt – flakes for crumbling over food at the table, coarse lumps for adding to cooking liquids. Lemon juice is freshly squeezed.

Moroccan preserved lemons (page 198) are one of my current favourite ingredients and crop up in several recipes. If you enjoy drinking *Margaritas* you'll probably like their flavour – it has a similar quality. They are very simple indeed to make and add a definite something extra to any dish in which they are used. That said, they have to stand around in the kitchen for at least seven days before they're usable, so if you don't have any to hand, simply use grated lemon zest instead.

Most vegetable stock powders and cubes taste pretty nasty. I've tried many, and the only one I can honestly recommend is Marigold Swiss Vegetable Bouillon Powder. I've used it for years because it actually taste of vegetables, unlike many of its rivals. It is quite easy to find, at least in British shops.

GROWING FOOD

I have a kitchen garden in which I grow some of my own fruit, vegetables and herbs. It's a great source of inspiration to me, and I find the whole process of growing food immensely rewarding and enjoyable. It's also hard work and time-consuming, so I don't grow as much as I'd ideally like to.

All the food in this book can be made perfectly well with shop-bought ingredients but, for any readers interested in growing food, there are a few pointers in the recipes to particular crops I have found especially useful and good to grow.

WEIGHTS, MEASURES, PRECISION AND EXPERIMENTATION

Experienced cooks will take the recipes as a starting point, adapting them to suit particular conditions and requirements, which is perfectly fine by me. Less experienced cooks will, I hope, appreciate the reassurance of tightly defined recipes. Although I've given precise measures so you can duplicate a specific end result, most recipes are quite forgiving if you decide to improvise.

A tablespoon is 15 ml, a teaspoon is 5 ml and spoonfuls are level unless otherwise stated. Where it matters I've given the exact dimensions of pots, pans and other cooking vessels. The size of such things can have a dramatic influence on cooking times and the way a recipe turns out. Liquids evaporate much faster from a wide, shallow pan than from a tall, narrow one, for example.

The recipes have all been test-cooked by someone other than myself, namely my husband, Andrew, to ensure that they *work* if followed accurately, but do treat them as a starting point if that's where you're at. Experiment if you feel like it, and trust your own taste and judgment. I hope that ultimately you're cooking to please yourself. There is no single right way to cook and only you should be the final arbiter.

PAINTINGS AND PRINTS

I have some niggling reservations about food photographs. Much as I enjoy them, a straw poll of friends and acquaintances revealed that for every person who finds them useful at least one other finds them intimidating. . . Hence the idea of a collaboration with an artist was born. I wanted to create a book in which the vividness and sensuality of the illustrations at least matched that of the food – a book that would inspire in the kitchen and also be a feast for the eyes – a beautiful object in itself. In Elda Abramson I found an artistic collaborator who exceeded even my most optimistic expectations. A selection of Elda's paintings from Vegetable Heaven are available as giclée prints in a range of sizes from **www.pauntley-prints.co.uk/vh**. For more information see Page 223.

ACKNOWLEDGMENTS

Heartfelt thanks to the following people who have helped in innumerable ways: Elda Abramson, Lynne Clark, Adam Flowers, Danny Flowers, Andrew Ford, Andrew Moss, Liz Oppedijk, Bernadette Stokoe.

· Catherine Mason

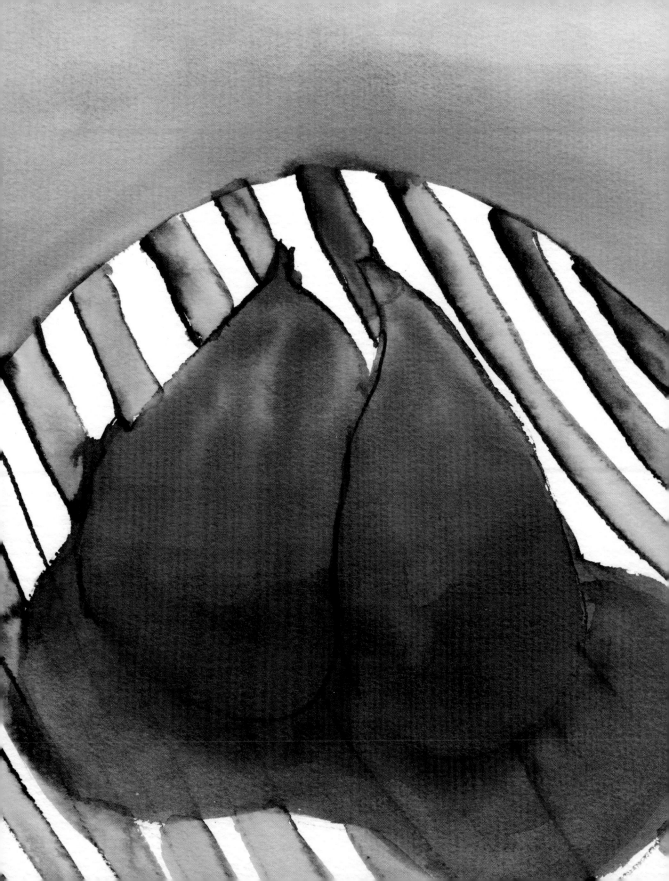

A WORD FROM THE ILLUSTRATOR

These things have a habit of coming out of the blue. When Catherine Mason phoned me and asked me if I would prepare sixty paintings to illustrate *Vegetable Heaven*, I was bowled over. For a start, the immensity of the project was breathtaking, but more than that, I wondered whether my style of painting was going to be right for it. I had acquired some small reputation for the Zen techniques I apply to flower painting, but – and I know this will sound odd – I had too little experience of vegetable painting to feel absolutely confident that my techniques would work for such very different subjects. I paint with inks and there are certain constraints in their use that make it hard to be certain in advance exactly how they will work with a given subject.

Then I met Catherine and I knew immediately that we could work together. Her knowledge of her subject, her enthusiasm for vegetarian cookery and her absolute conviction that she could deliver interesting, seductive, gourmet dishes was infectious. If she thought my work could complement that, I couldn't wait to get started.

I'd be lying if I didn't say it was tough. I had half guessed that trying to convey the sensual experience of good vegetarian cooking was not going to be easy, but I had underestimated the time it would take to get things right. For the paintings to work in a book like this, you try to capture the essence of what it is that makes the experience the recipe represents. Good food ravishes the senses. It is the combination of look, taste and smell that makes it special, so that is what you try to capture.

I work mostly at night. I do this because it's the time when the phone isn't ringing and I can concentrate on what I'm doing without distraction. *Vegetable Heaven* took more nights than I care to remember, as I realised that sixty paintings was probably only half of what I would have to do. Catherine had asked me for seventy so that she would have some choice, but I knew that that would not be enough. Not because I doubted my own work, but because with a project of this nature, it's important to get complete synergy between recipe and painting. And you only really know that you have achieved that when you start to assemble text and visuals together into a unified whole. So I created 142 paintings.

Now it's done, I look back on it with huge enjoyment. It's a wonderful project to have worked on and I only hope that readers get even half the enjoyment from this book that I have from working on it.

Elda Abramson

STARTERS, SOUPS AND SALADS

Caramelized red onion tartlets with rosemary

This is a lovely cold-weather starter. It's warm, soothing and savoury, light as air and tantalizingly fragrant. From the cook's point of view, it's ridiculously quick and easy to make. The onions are sliced so thinly they require no preliminary cooking, and will soften and caramelize in the oven. The tartlets are very light and insubstantial and should be followed by something quite hefty.

- 2 smallish red onions (about 220 g in total), peeled and sliced into wafer-thin rings
- 1 tablespoon olive oil
- 2 pinches sugar
- 2 sprigs rosemary, woody bits discarded, leaves chopped
- a little salt and pepper to season
- 1 sheet ready rolled puff pastry
- about 1 tablespoon milk
- 30–40 g grated fresh Parmesan cheese (optional)

Oven temperature: 220°C (425°F, gas 7) – adjust for fan ovens

1   Using your fingers, turn over the onions, oil, sugar, rosemary, salt and pepper together in a bowl until evenly mixed. Do this gently to avoid breaking up the onion rings too much.

2   Cut circles (or rectangles if you prefer) of pastry 10–12 cm in diameter, using either a pastry cutter or cutting around a saucer with a sharp knife. Place the pastries on a baking sheet and score with the tip of a sharp knife 8–9 mm in from the edge to form a rim. Don't cut right through the pastry. Prick over the central area of each pastry with a fork.

3   Share out the onions carefully in loose piles between the pastries, avoiding the rim area. Brush the bare pastry rims with a little milk, then bake on the middle shelf of the oven until crisp and golden, around 15 minutes. The tartlets will probably rise in the middle, but they sink again when they come out of the oven.

4   If you want to add Parmesan, sprinkle it over the pastries when they are cooked and return them to the oven for 1–2 minutes.

MAKES 3–4 TARTLETS

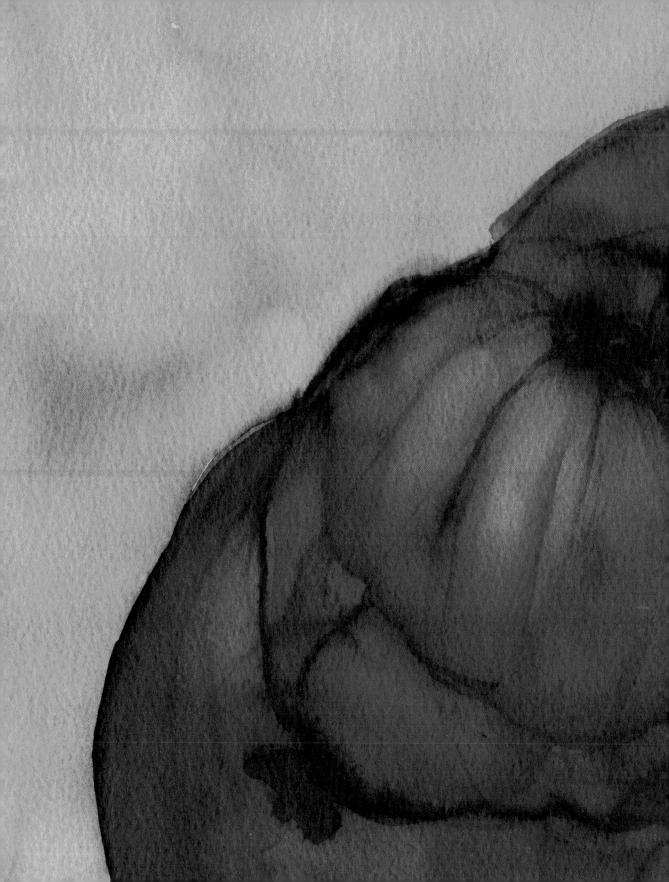

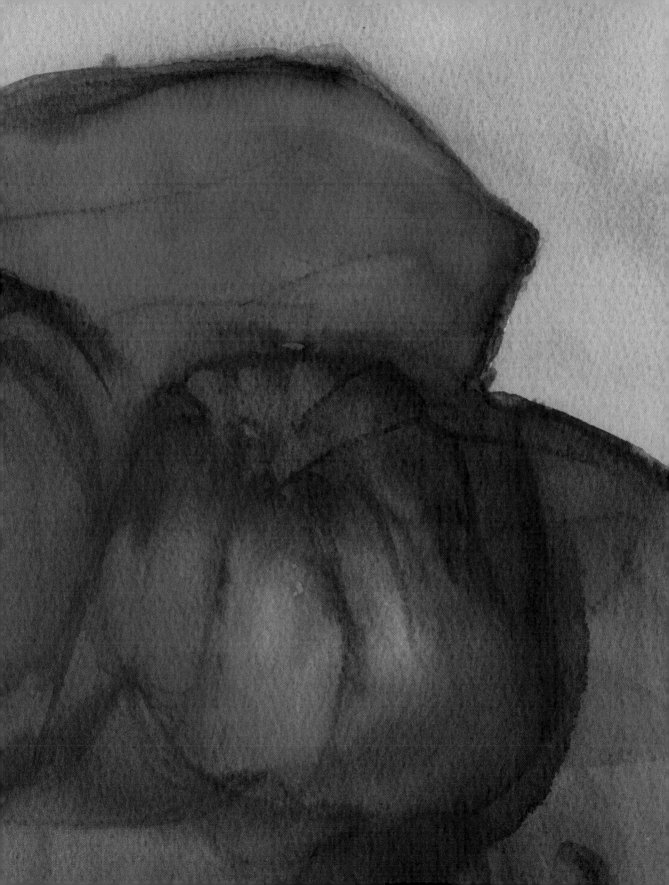

Spiced pumpkin dip

This is a tasty vegetable-based dip, relatively low in fat and quite light on the dairy products. Serve it with raw vegetables or tortilla chips as a casual starter or an accompaniment for drinks.

- 150 g *Roast caramelized butternut squash with tarragon* (page 117)
- 1 fresh red chilli pepper, finely chopped, or more to taste
- 2 tablespoons mayonnaise
- 1 tablespoon sun-dried tomato paste
- 60 g fresh Parmesan, finely grated
- salt and pepper to taste

1 Whiz all the ingredients together in a food processor until smooth. Check and adjust the seasoning if necessary. Depending on your preferences and their strength, you may want to add more chilli.

VARIATION
Omit the chilli pepper and add some chopped fresh tarragon.

Baked aubergine slices with pesto and red onions

Aubergines have the capacity to absorb huge amounts of oil, but this recipe uses quite a modest quantity without compromising on flavour. Individual aubergine slices are spread with a thin layer of pesto and topped with slices of red onion, before being baked in a single layer. They look very decorative when cooked. They would also make a lovely filling for a hot sandwich – spread a crusty roll with garlic mayonnaise first and add a few crunchy salad vegetables along with the hot aubergine slices.

- 1 large aubergine, sliced into 1 cm rings
- salt and pepper
- 2 tablespoons olive oil
- about 2 tablespoons pesto (shop-bought is fine here)
- 1 medium-sized red onion, peeled and thinly sliced into rings (you need the same number of onion slices as there are aubergine slices)
- 30 g fresh Parmesan curls (made with a potato peeler)

Oven temperature: 220°C (425°F, gas 7) – adjust for fan ovens

You will need a shallow, oven-proof gratin dish big enough to hold the aubergine slices in a single layer.

1 Sprinkle the aubergine slices with salt on both sides, then leave them in a colander, preferably in a single layer, to degorge for about 30 minutes. This salting process draws out any bitter juices and makes the aubergine less prone to soak up oil. Rinse the slices thoroughly in cold water, then drain and pat them dry with kitchen paper.

2 Brush some of the oil over the base of the gratin dish and place the aubergine slices in a single layer in the dish. Brush their upper surfaces with a little more oil. Season with salt and pepper. Put about half a teaspoon of pesto on each aubergine slice and spread evenly so the entire surface is thinly coated. Place an onion slice on each aubergine slice, then brush the remaining oil on the onions. Season the onions lightly with salt and pepper.

3 Cover the dish and bake in a pre-heated oven for 25 minutes, then take off the cover and cook for 10 minutes more. Sprinkle with the Parmesan curls and cook for another 5 minutes (40 minutes total).

SERVES 4 AS A STARTER

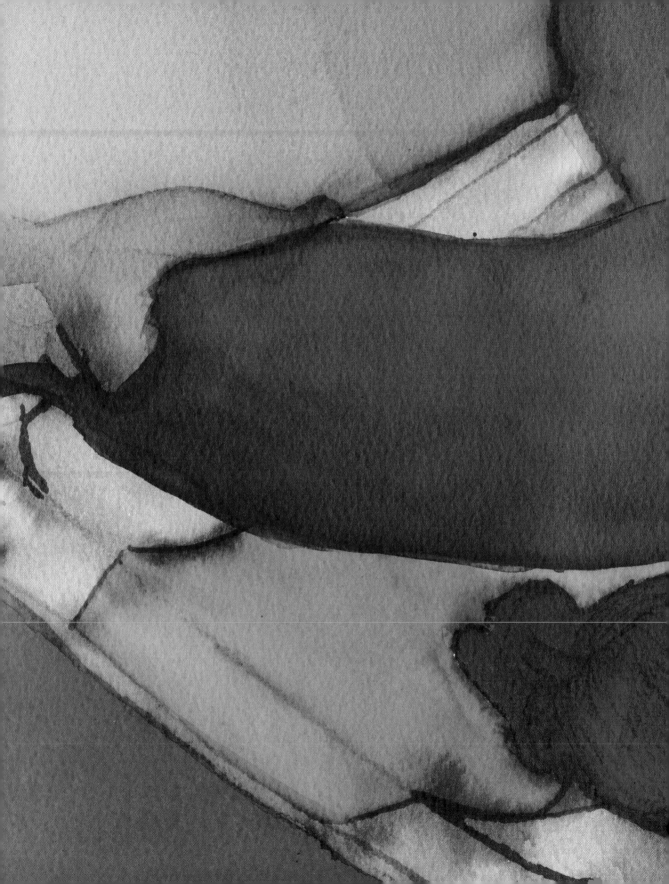

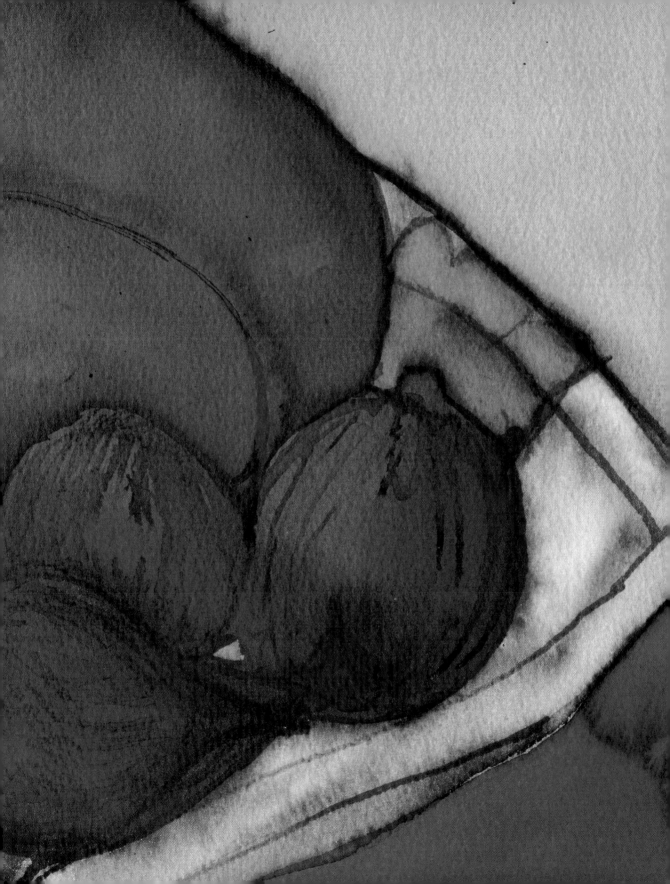

Roast pumpkin soup with Ancho chilli and lime

This smoky, spicy, colourful soup makes a perfect lunch for a cool autumn day. The dried Ancho chilli used to flavour this recipe is popular in Mexican cooking. Large, fruity, smoky and not too ferociously hot, it is an excellent ingredient, and can be found in Mexican food shops or the specialist food sections of the better supermarkets. If you can't find it, use a small amount of any fresh red chilli you can get hold of, added at stage 3 below.

- 15 g butter
- 2 tablespoons olive oil
- 650 g diced pumpkin or squash, weighed after preparation
- 400 g onions, peeled and roughly chopped
- 3 large cloves of garlic, peeled and left whole
- 1 dried Ancho chilli

- 900 ml well-flavoured vegetable stock
- 1 teaspoon salt
- 1 fresh lime, finely grated zest and juice
- 120 ml single cream
- 2 tablespoons (about 15 g) chopped fresh coriander leaves

Oven temperature: 220°C (425°F, gas 7) – adjust for fan ovens

1. Heat the oven and put the butter and olive oil in a large roasting tin in the oven to warm. When the butter has browned slightly, add the pumpkin, onions and garlic to the roasting tin, then stir to coat thoroughly. Cover with foil or a well-fitting lid and bake for about 30 minutes. Remove the foil and return the tin to the oven for a further 5 minutes to brown the vegetables and drive off some of the steam.

2. While the vegetables are roasting, deal with the chilli. Remove the stalk and seeds, then put it in the oven for 5 minutes to roast slightly – it brings out the fragrance. Remove the chilli from the oven, place it in a bowl and pour on boiling water. Leave it to soak for 20 minutes, then drain.

3. Put the roasted vegetables and soaked chilli in the food processor and whiz until smooth. If the purée is too stiff to mix easily, add a little of the vegetable stock. Add the salt, all the lime zest and about half the lime juice. Taste, and add more lime juice if necessary. Put the purée into a pan and gradually stir in the vegetable stock and cream. Heat, stirring, until the soup is warm, but don't let it boil. Stir in the coriander just before serving.

SERVES 4 FOR LUNCH, 6 AS A STARTER

Tomato and chickpea soup with saffron

This is a nice variation on tomato soup, quite suitable for a winter menu. I made it in February with frozen home-grown tomatoes and it seemed entirely appropriate – hearty enough for winter, but with a flavour that is a beautiful, haunting reminder of late summer. If you don't have any well-flavoured fresh (or frozen) tomatoes, canned plum tomatoes make an acceptable substitute.

- 15 g butter
- 1 tablespoon olive oil
- 2 medium onions, peeled and chopped
- 4 cloves of garlic, peeled and chopped
- 3 smallish potatoes, peeled and cut into 1 cm chunks
- 1 kg fresh, ripe tomatoes, peeled and chopped
- a generous pinch of saffron threads
- 400 g can chickpeas, drained
- 2 heaped teaspoons sun-dried tomato paste
- vegetable stock
- milk, cream or creamed coconut (optional, as preferred)
- a teaspoon or two of lemon juice, freshly squeezed
- salt and pepper

1   Heat the butter and olive oil gently in a large soup pan. Add the onions and fry gently for a few minutes until it starts to soften. Add the garlic and potatoes, then fry for a few minutes more. Stir in the tomatoes and saffron, bring the pan to the boil, cover and simmer gently for 45 minutes to 1 hour, until all the vegetables are perfectly tender.

2   Tip about two thirds of the chickpeas into the food processor. Use a slotted spoon to transfer about half the vegetables from the cooked soup to the food processor bowl on top of the chick peas. Process to a smooth purée and stir back into the soup pan. The idea is to thicken the soup but retain some of its chunky texture. Add the remaining whole chickpeas to the soup, then stir in the sun-dried tomato paste.

3   Re-heat the soup gently and thin with some well-flavoured vegetable stock to the desired consistency. The quantity will vary according to individual prefer-ence, the wateriness of the tomatoes, etc, so add the stock in increments, taste as you go and use your own judgment.

4   You may also want to enrich the soup with milk, cream or creamed coconut, although it will still taste delicious if you choose to omit this step. As with the stock, add these little by little and taste as you go. If you're adding creamed coconut, aim for enough to make the soup creamy but not so much that the flavour comes through discernibly. Finally, add lemon juice, salt and pepper until the soup is to your liking. Trust your taste buds! If you like it the chances are that others will, too.

SERVES 6 AS A STARTER, 3 OR 4 FOR LUNCH

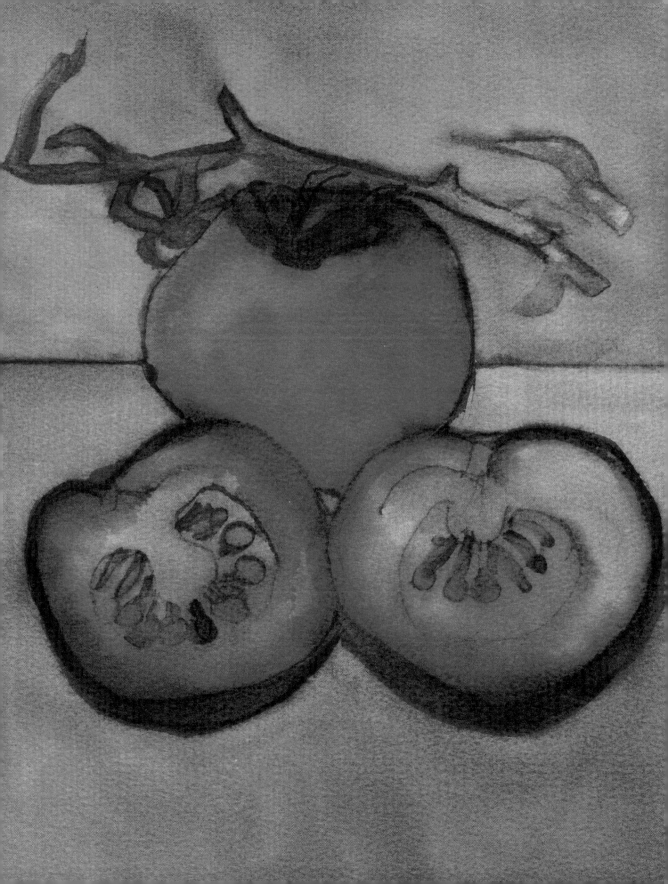

Carrot and coconut soup

This is a useful vegan soup, although it can't in truth be described as low fat due to the coconut milk. The addition of mint was a lucky accident. I had intended to make carrot and coriander soup, and cooking was well underway before I realized I didn't have any coriander in the house or garden. I used fresh mint instead and was delighted with the result.

- 2 tablespoons olive oil
- 3 medium onions, peeled and roughly chopped
- 1 kg carrots, peeled and roughly chopped
- 250 g potatoes, peeled and chopped
- 30 g piece of fresh ginger root, peeled and finely chopped
- 2–3 large, mild red chillies, de-seeded and finely chopped
- 2 stalks lemon grass, bashed with a blunt instrument but left whole
- 4 cloves garlic, peeled and chopped
- 1 litre vegetable stock
- about 15 g fresh mint leaves
- 400 ml coconut milk
- juice of half a lemon
- salt and pepper

1 Warm the oil in a large soup pan. Add the onions, carrots, potatoes, ginger, chillies, lemon grass and garlic and fry gently for about 5 minutes. Pour on the stock, bring the soup to the boil, then turn the heat down quite low. Simmer for about 30 minutes until all the vegetables are very tender, then fish out and discard the lemon grass.

2 Purée the soup in a food processor, in batches if necessary. You could add the mint leaves at this stage and avoid having to chop them by hand. Return the soup to the rinsed-out pan and re-heat, adding the coconut milk and lemon juice. Taste and adjust the seasoning to your liking.

SERVES 6 AS A STARTER, 3 OR 4 FOR LUNCH

Sweetcorn and butternut chowder

Warming and cheerful in autumn or winter, this is a big soup, and rather heavy on the veg prep, but it's one of those recipes where it's almost as easy to make a lot as a little. It will keep quite happily in the fridge for a few days, but if the quantity given below is still too much it's easy enough to make half.

- 6 fat cobs of fresh sweetcorn or 500 g frozen kernels
- 15 g butter
- 2 tablespoons olive oil
- 2 large onions, peeled and chopped
- 4 stalks of celery, finely chopped
- 4 medium-sized carrots, peeled and chopped
- 1 large red pepper, de-seeded, de-veined and diced
- 1 large or 2 medium potatoes, peeled and diced quite small
- a Butternut squash weighing around 700 g before preparation, peeled, de-seeded and cut into 1 cm dice
- 4 cloves garlic, peeled and finely chopped
- ½ Habanero chilli, or 2–3 of a milder sort, de-seeded and finely chopped
- 1½ litres vegetable stock
- 200 g crème fraîche
- salt and pepper
- about 2 teaspoons Champagne vinegar or fresh lemon juice
- coarsely chopped fresh coriander leaves to garnish (around 15 g)

1 If using fresh corn, tug off the surrounding leaves, strip the kernels from the cobs with the aid of a small sharp knife and set them aside for later.

2 Warm the butter and olive oil together in a large pan, turn the heat down quite low and sweat the onions, celery, carrots, red pepper and potatoes for about 10 minutes. Add the squash, garlic and chillies and cook about 5 minutes more.

3 Pour in the vegetable stock, cover the pan and simmer everything for about 20 minutes until all the vegetables are quite tender. Add the prepared corn kernels, bring the pan back to the boil and simmer for a further 4–5 minutes, just long enough to cook the corn.

4 Now you have a choice of methods for thickening the chowder. Either use a potato masher and mash some of the vegetables directly in the soup pan, or use a slotted spoon to decant some of the vegetables into a blender or food processor and purée them, then stir them back into the chowder. The plan is to thicken the matrix, but still retain quite a lot of texture in the chowder.

5 When you're happy with the consistency, stir in the crème fraîche and re-heat. Check for seasoning. You may need to add extra salt if your stock was not very salty, and you'll certainly need a good grinding of black pepper. A splash of Champagne vinegar or fresh lemon juice added now will brighten the flavours without overpowering them. Stir in the coriander leaves just before serving.

SERVES 8 FOR LUNCH, 10 OR MORE AS A STARTER

Broad bean patties

These tasty little patties are a variation on the falafel theme. Pale green on the inside with a crisp, brown crust, they are equally successful made with fresh or frozen beans. Serve them with some mixed, dressed salad leaves and with a wedge of lemon, a sauce such as *Smoked garlic and saffron mayonnaise* (page 201) or a dish of cool, minty yogurt.

- 500 g broad beans, prepared weight (900 g fresh pods should be enough to yield this amount)
- 2 cloves of garlic, peeled and crushed
- 5–6 spring onions, coarsely chopped, including some green
- 1 teaspoon ground cumin seeds
- 1 teaspoon ground coriander seeds
- 2–3 tablespoons finely chopped fresh savory or parsley leaves
- 1 small egg (or slightly less), beaten lightly
- salt and pepper
- light olive oil for frying

1   Simmer fresh broad beans in salted water for 5–10 minutes until tender (for frozen beans follow the instructions on the packet). Drain and allow them to cool slightly, then put the beans, garlic, spring onions, cumin, coriander and savory in a food processor. Purée until smooth, stopping the machine and scraping the mixture down from the sides as necessary. As the skins are quite fibrous you'll need to run the food processor for a few minutes.

2   Gradually add the beaten egg by pouring it through the spout while the machine is running. You may not need all the egg – just add enough to bind the mixture. If you make the mixture too wet the patties will be fragile. Taste the mixture and adjust the seasoning.

3   Heat 2–3 tablespoons of olive oil in a wide shallow frying pan. Drop dessert-spoonfuls of the mixture gently into the hot oil, flatten slightly with the back of the spoon and fry without disturbing them for 3–4 minutes, until the underneath is crisp. Turn them over carefully using a thin spatula and fry the other sides for 2–3 minutes. Drain, blot the patties on kitchen paper and serve immediately.

SERVES 4

Green bean, olive and lemon salad

This is a very tasty way of serving choice young beans fresh from the garden in summer. The *Moroccan preserved lemons* (page 198) definitely add a certain something, but don't worry if you don't have any – simply substitute a chunk of un-peeled, well-scrubbed, fresh organic lemon and a little extra salt. Served with some fresh Somerset goat's cheese and decent bread this salad makes a lovely, simple warm-weather lunch.

- 450 g small runner or French beans, trimmed
- 1 tablespoon finely-chopped red onion
- 8 Kalamata olives, stoned and cut into rings
- ⅛ preserved lemon, finely chopped (see above)
- 1 clove of garlic, peeled and crushed
- 3 tablespoons olive oil
- freshly-squeezed lemon juice, to taste (about ⅓ of a lemon's worth)
- salt and pepper

1 Cook the beans in plenty of boiling salted water until just tender (3–5 minutes). Meanwhile put the onion, olives, preserved lemon, garlic and olive oil into the salad bowl and mix together.

2 As soon as the beans are cooked, drain and add them to the salad bowl, swirling them around so they are well-coated with the dressing ingredients. Add the lemon juice, salt and pepper to your liking, tasting as you go. Serve while still slightly warm.

SERVES 3–4

Roast pepper and red onion salad with preserved lemon

These flavoured, roasted vegetables make an easy and versatile salad, which is equally good served warm or cold. They also make a good sandwich filling, either alone or with a few slivers of salty feta cheese. They will keep in the fridge for several days. If you don't have any preserved lemons, you might like to add 3 or 4 branches of rosemary to the roasting pan instead.

- 2 tablespoons olive oil
- ⅛ preserved lemon (page 198), finely chopped
- 1 tablespoon balsamic vinegar
- ½ teaspoon salt
- 750 g mixed red and orange peppers, de-seeded and quartered
- 4 small red onions, peeled and cut lengthwise into eighths

Oven temperature: 220°C (425°F, gas 7) – adjust for fan ovens

1 Put the olive oil, preserved lemon, balsamic vinegar and salt in a wide, shallow roasting tin and stir them together. Add the peppers and onions, stir well and distribute the vegetables evenly so they're more or less in a single layer.

2 Roast uncovered for about 30 minutes, until tender, turning the vegetables about half way through the cooking time. Allow the salad to cool for at least 10 minutes before serving. It tastes equally good warm or cold, but not piping hot.

SERVES 4

MAIN COURSES

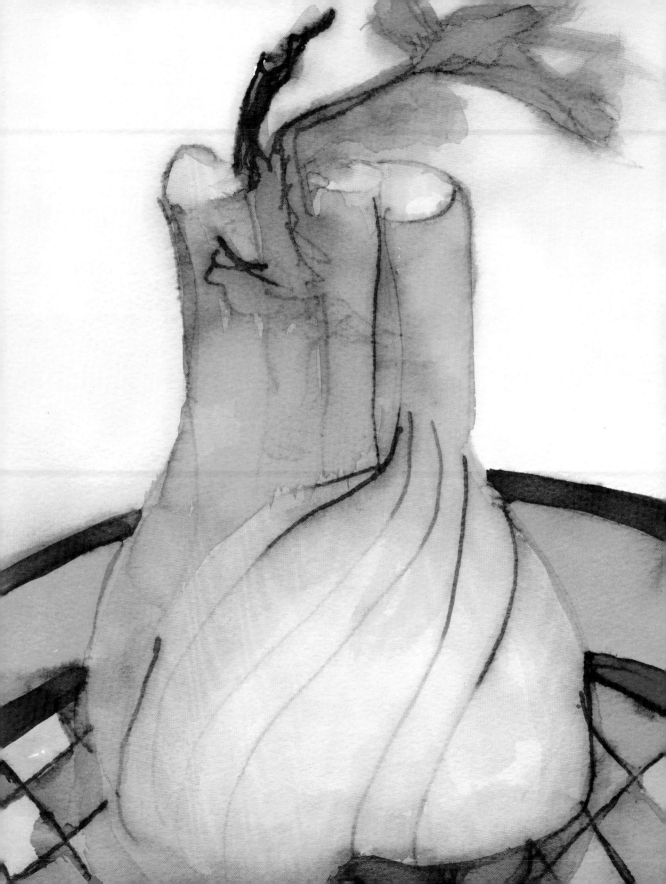

Fennel tart with dolcelatte and verjuice

Fennel is a lovely and much under-used vegetable, distinctive enough to stand more or less alone. This tart is very easy, especially if you use shop-bought, ready rolled pastry, and may be served hot or lukewarm.

Verjuice, the unfermented juice of wine grapes, was commonly used in medieval cooking. It is enjoying something of a revival and may now be found in at least one major supermarket chain. More sour in flavour than the sweet grape juice sold for drinking, it is good for adding a not-too-acidic tang to many savoury dishes. If you can't get hold of it you could substitute a half-and-half mixture of sweet white grape juice and fresh lemon juice (or even just the juice of a single lemon) to good effect.

- 500 g fennel bulbs, crisp and white
- 15 g butter
- 1 tablespoon olive oil
- 1 teaspoon fennel seeds
- 100 ml verjuice (see above)
- 1 sheet ready rolled shortcrust pastry (about 35 cm diameter)
- salt and pepper
- 150–200 g dolcelatte cheese

Oven temperature: 220°C (425°F, gas 7) – adjust for fan ovens

1   Trim the fennel and cut it into segments lengthwise – into quarters if your bulbs are very small, otherwise into eighths. Warm the butter and olive oil in a heavy frying pan, and fry the fennel over a moderate heat until it starts to brown. Add the fennel seeds and verjuice, cover the pan and simmer for 15–20 minutes until the fennel is tender. Take off the lid and, if much liquid remains, allow it to cook off. Remove the pan from the heat and set aside.

2   While the fennel is cooking unroll the pastry onto a large metal baking sheet. Fold over a 1 cm rim all the way round the edge and crimp the pastry between forefinger and thumb to make a decorative edge. Prick all over the inside of the pastry case with a fork, then bake it blind for 10 minutes.

3   Arrange the cooked fennel over the part-cooked pastry case and season with salt and pepper. Dot generous cubes of cheese over the fennel and return the tart to the oven for about 10 minutes, until the cheese has melted invitingly and the top is golden and bubbling.

SERVES 4

Spinach and mushroom pie topped with parsley mash

Warming comfort food for a cold autumn or winter evening, this is a one-dish supper and is one of those useful recipes requiring no last minute preparation.

THE SPINACH AND MUSHROOM LAYER

- 15 g butter
- 1 tablespoon olive oil
- 1 small onion, peeled and finely chopped
- 200 g mushrooms, cut into chunks
- 180 g cleaned spinach
- 3 cloves garlic, peeled and finely chopped
- juice of half a lemon
- salt and pepper
- 120 g creamy Gorgonzola, cut into hefty chunks
- 1 tablespoon finely chopped fresh parsley

THE PARSLEY MASH LAYER

- 400–450 g plain mashed potato
- 1 tablespoon finely chopped fresh parsley
- 1 egg, lightly beaten
- 30–40 g fresh Parmesan cheese, grated
- 2 tablespoons milk
- salt and pepper

Oven temperature: 220°C (425°F, gas 7) – adjust for fan ovens

THE SPINACH AND MUSHROOM LAYER

1 Warm the oil and butter in a heavy frying pan. Fry the onions and mushrooms gently, stirring from time to time. When they are just about tender, add the spinach and garlic and cook, stirring until the spinach is just wilted. Add the lemon juice and season with salt and pepper.

2 Remove the pan from the heat and allow it to cool slightly before stirring in the Gorgonzola and parsley. The mixture should be cool enough so as not to melt the cheese at this point. Spread the mixture evenly in an oven-proof dish (22 cm diameter by 7 cm deep).

THE PARSLEY MASH LAYER

1 If you don't happen to have mashed potato left over from another meal just boil or steam the potatoes and mash them in your usual way. Add the remaining mash ingredients to the potato and beat until smooth. Taste and adjust the seasoning if necessary. Spread the topping over the mushroom spinach layer and ruffle up the surface with a fork. Bake for 20–30 minutes in the pre-heated oven until the top is golden brown and bubbling. Allow to rest for 5 minutes before serving.

SERVES 2–3

Tomato feta tart with basil

This tart can be put together very quickly indeed, especially if you use ready rolled pastry. I used to be rather sniffy about it but, having tried it, I had to admit it tasted just as good as my own home-made pastry, and it's certainly a lot less hassle to prepare.

Excellent if made with ripe, late-summer tomatoes, the tart's success hinges on the tomatoes being very well-flavoured so, if in doubt, use cherry tomatoes, which can generally be relied upon to taste of something. They also look rather pretty in this dish, but it's fine made with larger tomatoes, too.

- 1 sheet ready rolled shortcrust pastry
- 2–3 tablespoons pesto (shop-bought is fine)
- about 300 g ripe cherry tomatoes, halved (or larger tomatoes cut into chunks)
- salt and pepper
- a little balsamic vinegar
- 100–120 g Greek feta cheese, crumbled
- 6 to 10 fresh basil leaves

Oven temperature: 220°C (425°F, gas 7) – adjust for fan ovens

1 Place the pastry on a large baking sheet and fold over a 1 cm rim around the edge. Crimp the rim with your fingers, so it stands up slightly. Prick the bottom of the pastry case all over with a fork and bake for 8–10 minutes. Remove the pastry case from the oven (press it gently with the back of a spoon if it shows signs of rising up in the middle).

2 Spread the pesto over the part-cooked pastry case and top with the tomatoes. Try to arrange them in a single layer so they are mostly skin-side down, as this will help stop the pastry going soggy.

3 Season with salt, pepper and a very light sprinkling of balsamic vinegar, then put the tart in the oven for another 10 minutes to drive off some of the moisture from the tomatoes.

4 Sprinkle over the crumbled feta and cook for another 15–25 minutes, until the cheese is starting to brown. Allow to cool for at least 10 minutes and sprinkle with torn basil leaves before serving.

SERVES 4, WITH POTATOES AND A SALAD

Potato, red onion and ricotta tart with lovage and parsley

A tart for the masses, this is intensely savoury and useful for feeding a crowd, but the quantities can be halved quite easily if necessary.

- 2 tablespoons olive oil
- 500 g new potatoes, sliced as thinly as possible
- 1 clove garlic, peeled and chopped
- 4 tablespoons freshly chopped parsley and lovage, half and half
- ¾ teaspoon salt
- 500 g red onions, peeled and sliced into wafer-thin rings

- 1½ teaspoons sherry vinegar
- 2 sheets of ready rolled shortcrust pastry, defrosted if necessary
- 2 large eggs, lightly beaten
- 250 g ricotta cheese
- salt and pepper to taste
- 4–5 tablespoons milk
- 40 g fresh Parmesan cheese, coarsely grated

Oven temperature: 200°C (400°F, gas 6) – adjust for fan ovens

1 Warm 1 tablespoon of the olive oil in a heavy frying pan. Add the sliced potatoes and fry briefly, stirring them around so the oil is evenly distributed. Add the garlic and 1 tablespoon of the parsley and lovage mixture, stir again and add about 3–4 tablespoons water and half a teaspoon of salt to the pan. Cover and simmer for 8–9 minutes until the potatoes are tender. Remove the lid and cook off any remaining liquid, then turn into a dish and set aside to cool.

2 Scrape out any bits of potato sticking to the frying pan, add another tablespoon of olive oil and heat it for a moment. Add the red onion rings and fry for a couple of minutes. Add a pinch of salt and the sherry vinegar. Continue to cook, stirring occasionally, until the onions are tender. Try not to break up the rings too much. Set aside while you deal with the pastry.

3 Lay each sheet of pastry on a large metal baking tray and fold a rim all the way around the edge, about 1 cm wide. Crimp it using fingers and thumb to make slightly raised, decorative edges and prick the base all over with a fork. Brush each pastry case with a little beaten egg and put them into the oven for 10 minutes to set the egg and make a sog-proof barrier for the filling.

4 Meanwhile mix the rest of the beaten egg with the ricotta cheese and season to taste with salt and pepper. Thin the mixture with a few tablespoons of milk if it seems very stiff. Stir in about three quarters of the chopped fresh herbs, reserving a scattering for later.

5 Remove the part-cooked pastry cases from the oven and share out the potato slices evenly between them. Scatter the onion rings over the potatoes, then pour on the egg and cheese mixture. Scatter the Parmesan over the surface of the tarts, then bake for about 25 minutes until the top is golden brown and set. Just before serving sprinkle with the reserved green herbs. Serve the tart lukewarm or cold. A slight cooling period allows the flavours to develop.

SERVES 8 AS A MAIN COURSE, 12 AS A STARTER OR LIGHT LUNCH

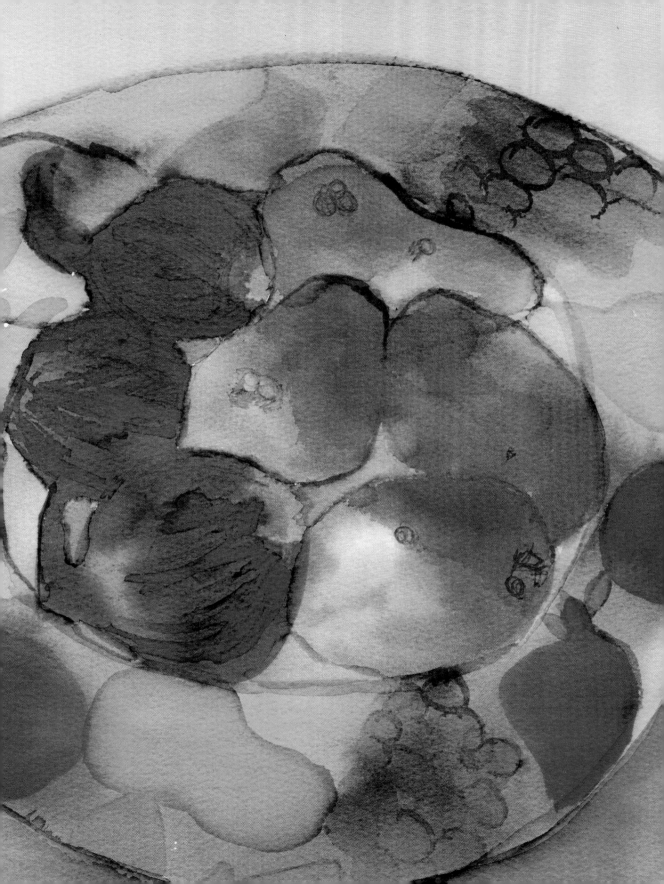

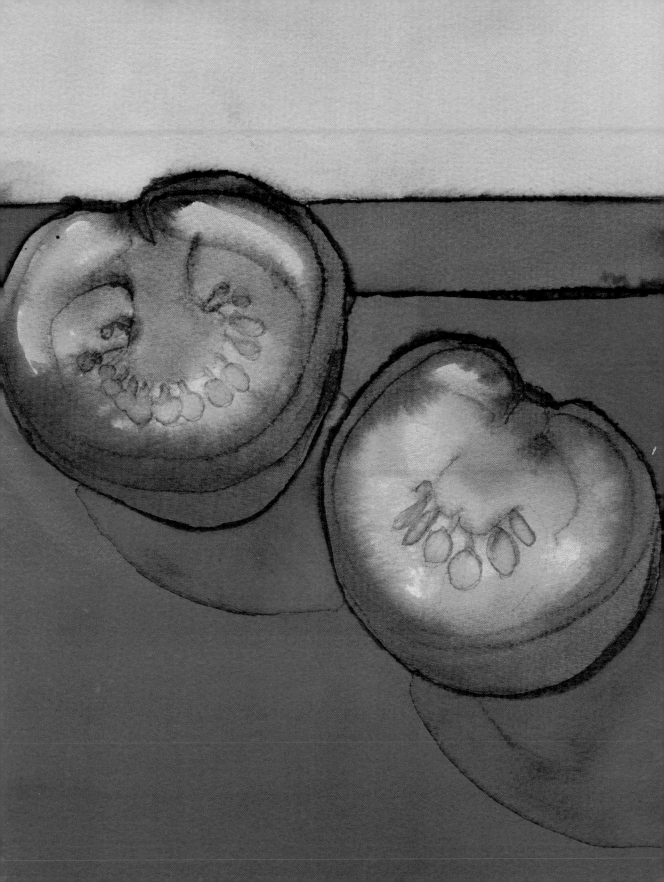

Spinach and tomato tart with Mascarpone

This tart, although something of a geographical hybrid, is exceptionally tasty and easy to put together. I generally speed up the proceedings by using pre-washed supermarket spinach. If you don't have any preserved lemons use some grated fresh lemon rind instead. The preserved lemons (page 198) are very worth having and easy to make, but they take a few days to mature.

- 1 sheet ready rolled shortcrust pastry
- 180 g spinach
- 15 g butter
- 1 tablespoon olive oil
- 1/8 preserved lemon (page 198), finely chopped
- salt and pepper
- 3 heaped teaspoons pesto (shop-bought is fine here)
- 3 hefty ripe tomatoes cut into chunks
- 2 tablespoons sun-dried tomato paste
- a clove of garlic, peeled and crushed
- 125 g Mascarpone or other soft, creamy cheese

Oven temperature: 200°C (400°F, gas 6) – adjust for fan ovens

1 Put the pastry on a metal baking sheet, fold over a rim around the edge, crimp it, prick the base all over with a fork and bake blind for 15 minutes.

2 Meanwhile, cook the spinach in the butter and olive oil in a wide shallow pan over a moderate heat for 2–3 minutes. Stir in the lemon and season with salt and pepper. Pile the cooked spinach onto a chopping board and chop coarsely. If much watery liquid remains in the pan, put it back on the heat for a couple of minutes to evaporate, then turn the heat off and put the spinach back in the pan with the remaining buttery juices.

3 Spread the partially cooked pastry base with pesto and dot the spinach around it in little piles. Scatter the tomato chunks into the gaps between the spinach.

4 Mix the tomato paste and garlic into the Mascarpone and season with salt and pepper. Drop spoonfuls of the cheese mixture over the surface of the tart. Put it back in the oven for about 10 minutes, until the cheese has melted and browned. Cool slightly before serving.

SERVES 4

Beetroot and potato tart with horseradish and Roquefort

A fragrant, savoury tart, equally good served warm or cool, this could be either a main course or a starter. All the vegetables could be prepared and cooked ahead of time if more convenient.

To prepare fresh beetroot, wash the roots thoroughly but don't peel them. Don't pierce the skin or trim the roots or shoots, as this makes them bleed during cooking. The leaves can be twisted off at about 5 cm. If the leaves are in good condition, don't throw them out but cook them like spinach – they are very tasty. Raw beetroot can be simmered in water or wrapped in foil and baked in the oven. Cooking times vary greatly but, as a guide, start testing boiled beetroot after about 45 minutes, baked after about an hour. The oven temperature is not critical and can be varied to suit whatever else is being cooked. Beetroots are done when they yield slightly to finger pressure. If you don't want to use them immediately they are best stored un-peeled in a sealed food container in the fridge.

- 1 sheet ready rolled shortcrust pastry
- 3 heaped teaspoons creamed horseradish
- 2–3 small salad potatoes, washed and cut into bite-sized chunks
- 2 small onions, peeled and cut lengthwise into wedges about the size of an orange segment
- 2–3 beetroots, boiled or baked in their skins until tender
- salt and pepper
- 120 g Roquefort cheese
- 15 g butter, melted

Oven temperature: 220°C (425°F, gas 7) – adjust for fan ovens

1 Put the pastry on a metal baking sheet, fold over and crimp a 1 cm rim around the edge. Prick the pastry all over with a fork (to stop it rising in the middle) and bake the empty case on the middle shelf in a pre-heated oven for 10 minutes. Remove from the oven and spread the creamed horseradish over the base. You may need to dilute it with a small amount of extra cream or hot water.

2 Simmer the potato chunks in salted water until they are just tender (5–8 minutes), adding the onion wedges to the potato cooking water for the last 2–3 minutes of this time. Drain the potatoes and onions thoroughly.

3 Peel the cooked beetroot and cut into wedges or chunks, as you prefer. Arrange the potatoes, onions and beetroots close together in a single layer on the pastry. Leave the beetroot till last, otherwise it will stain the spuds and onions. Season with salt and pepper, and crumble the cheese over the tart using your fingers.

4 Use a pastry brush and dab the melted butter onto any exposed areas of vegetable that are not directly covered with cheese. Put the tart back in the oven for a further 10–15 minutes, until browned and bubbling.

SERVES 4 AS A MAIN COURSE, 8 AS A STARTER

Spring vegetable and cashew stir-fry with chilli, basil and coconut sauce

A lively stir-fry for a spring day, making the most of the new vegetables as they come into season, this dish is a spring tonic, just bursting with vitality. Serve it with noodles or plainly-cooked Thai fragrant rice. The sauce is versatile and may be used with any combination of stir-fried vegetables.

As always with stir-fries, finish all the vegetable preparation before you start to cook, since the actual cooking takes only 5 minutes in total! The vegetables are added to the wok at timed intervals according to how long they take to cook and, as the timings are quite fine, it is helpful but not essential to use a stop watch. If you're making this single-handed it's also a good idea to cook the rice first and keep it warm while you stir-fry, to avoid last minute panics.

THE SAUCE

- 1 tablespoon groundnut oil
- a thumb-sized piece of fresh ginger or galangal, peeled and finely chopped
- 4 cloves garlic, peeled and finely chopped
- 1 large onion, peeled and finely chopped
- 1 or 2 hot red chillies, such as *Birds Eye*, de-seeded and sliced into wafer-thin rings
- 2 teaspoons palm sugar (ordinary brown sugar will do at a pinch)
- finely grated zest and juice of 1 lime
- ½ teaspoon salt
- 400 ml can coconut milk

THE STIR-FRY

- 2 tablespoons groundnut oil
- 60 g cashew nuts
- 70 g baby carrots, quartered lengthwise
- 150 g asparagus, peeled if thick, trimmed and cut into slanting 1 cm chunks
- 70 g baby sweetcorn, halved lengthwise
- 70 g mangetout or sugar-snap peas, topped and tailed
- bunch of spring onions, trimmed and sliced diagonally
- about 15 g fresh basil leaves, coarsely shredded
- light soy sauce to serve

THE SAUCE

Heat 1 tablespoon of the groundnut oil in a small saucepan and fry the chopped ginger, garlic and onion for a few minutes until sizzling and aromatic. Add the fresh chillies and fry for a couple of minutes longer, then add the palm sugar, lime juice, lime zest and salt. Pour in the coconut milk and simmer gently for 12–15 minutes, then keep the sauce warm while you stir-fry.

2 Heat 1 tablespoon of the groundnut oil in a wok over a moderate heat and stir-fry the cashews until evenly browned. Remove the nuts from the oil and set aside for later. Add the remaining oil to the wok and place on a high heat. Throw in the carrots and stir-fry for 1 minute. Add the asparagus and stir-fry for 1 minute more, then add the baby sweetcorn and mangetout peas and stir-fry for a further 3 minutes.

3 Check the vegetables and, if any of them still seem too hard, put a lid on the wok, turn the heat down quite low and let them cook in their own steam for a couple of minutes until just tender. Turn the heat back up to high, add the spring onions and stir-fry for 20 seconds.

4 Take the wok away from the heat and pour the sauce into it, adding the shredded basil and fried cashew nuts just before serving. Taste and add salt or light soy sauce if needed, then serve immediately on hot noodles or rice.

SERVES 2

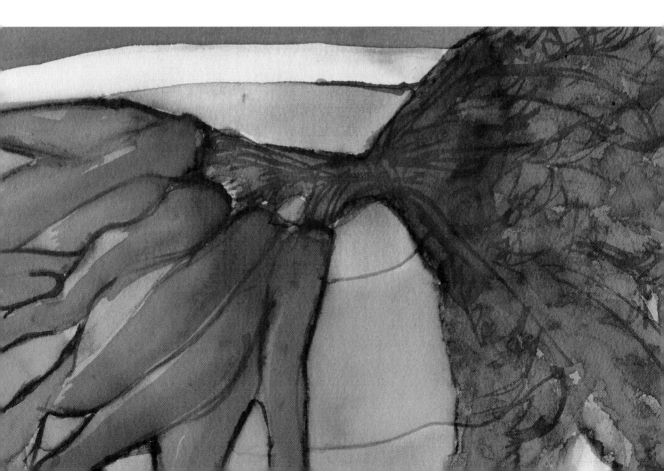

Fried spinach and chickpeas with lovage and cream

This dish makes a very quick and delicious supper, particularly speedy as I use a bag of pre-washed spinach from the supermarket and canned chickpeas. It is good served with hot bread, especially the *Lovage and onion bread* on page 175.

I extolled the virtues of lovage in *VEG*, my last book, and my opinion of it remains high. It's a fantastically savoury, intense herb, and very easy to grow, although not easy to find as a cut herb in the shops. Plants may be found in most garden centres and, being perennial, they come up year after year. One plant is generally ample for all but the largest households and the leaves freeze very successfully for winter use.

- 15 g (½ oz) butter
- 1 tablespoon olive oil
- 2 onions, peeled and finely sliced
- 4 cloves garlic, peeled and sliced
- 1 400 g can of chickpeas, drained
- ⅛ preserved lemon (page 198), finely chopped, or the finely grated rind from 1 fresh lemon
- 180 g spinach, coarsely chopped if the leaves are big
- 2 tablespoons chopped lovage leaves (parsley is an acceptable substitute)
- 120 ml cream
- salt and pepper

1   Warm the butter and olive oil in a large frying pan over a moderate heat. Fry the onions in this mixture until they are quite soft.

2   Add the garlic and chickpeas and fry for a while longer, until the chickpeas just start to brown. Add the preserved lemon or lemon rind. Stir, then add the spinach. Cover the pan and allow the spinach to wilt for 2–3 minutes, until just tender.

3   Stir in the lovage and cream, heat through for a moment or two, then season to taste with salt and pepper and serve immediately, with plenty of warm bread to mop up the juices.

SERVES 2

Chickpeas with spinach and potatoes

Slightly less rich than the spinach and chickpea recipe opposite, this is still a very tasty and quick supper dish, especially quick if you use ready-prepared spinach. Unless the spinach leaves are enormous there's no need to chop them.

- 400 g potatoes, peeled, cut into bite-sized chunks and boiled in salted water for about 8 minutes until tender
- 1 large red onion, peeled and chopped
- 15 g butter
- 1 tablespoon olive oil
- 400 g can chickpeas, drained
- 1 or 2 red chilli peppers (according to strength), de-seeded and finely chopped
- 3 heaped teaspoons sun-dried tomato paste
- juice of half a lemon
- 180 g spinach, washed and drained
- salt and pepper
- 60–90 g fresh Parmesan cheese, grated
- 2 tablespoons chopped parsley

1 If you don't have any pre-cooked potatoes to hand put some on to boil before doing anything else.

2 Fry the onion in the butter and olive oil in a wide, heavy pan until tender. Add the chickpeas and chilli and fry a couple of minutes longer. Add the tomato paste and lemon juice, stir well and add the spinach and pre-cooked potatoes. Season with salt and pepper. Cook, stirring, for about 5 minutes until the spinach is tender.

3 Sprinkle over the Parmesan and parsley and put a lid on the pan for a couple of minutes until the cheese has melted.

SERVES 2

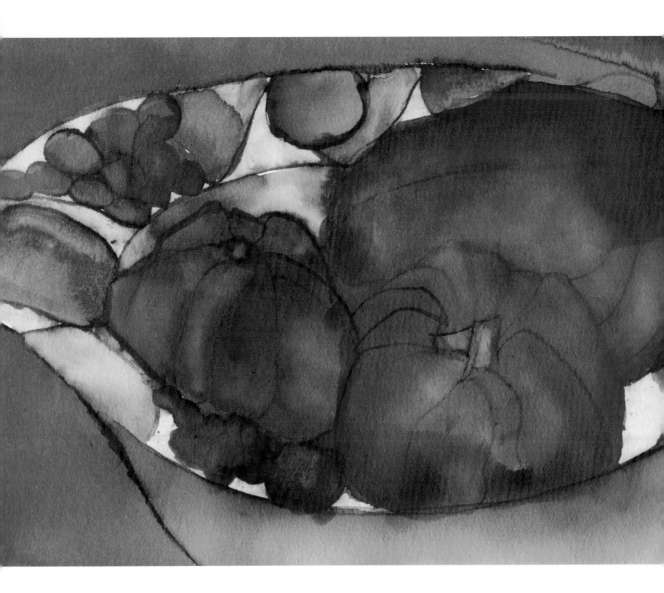

Pumpkin stew with coconut, chilli and coriander

This savoury autumnal stew is very quick and easy to make. Use floury potatoes and dice them quite small (1–2 cm) so they more or less disintegrate and thicken the stew when cooked. They should virtually disappear, giving you the excuse to serve this dish with more potatoes, mashed, baked or roasted, should you so desire. Good, rib-sticking, cold-weather comfort food, it's also a cheerful colour for a grey day.

- 1 large or 2 small butternut or other well-flavoured squash or pumpkin, weighing about 1½ kg in total
- 1 tablespoon olive oil
- 4 onions, peeled and chopped
- 4 cloves garlic, peeled and thinly sliced
- 4 red chillies, de-seeded and finely chopped
- 400 g potatoes, peeled and cut into 1 cm dice
- 250 ml vegetable stock
- 400 ml can of coconut milk
- salt and pepper
- a generous bunch of fresh coriander leaves, coarsely chopped

1   Cut the squash in half from top to bottom and scoop out the seeds. Place each half cut-side down and slice into semi-circles, about 2 cm wide. Slice off the skin from each piece and cut the flesh into 2 cm dice.

2   Warm the oil in a large pan and fry the onions for about 3 minutes, stirring occasionally. Add the garlic, chillies, potatoes and squash and fry for a couple of minutes more.

3   Pour in the stock and coconut milk, bring the contents of the pan to the boil, then turn down the heat and simmer, covered, for 15–20 minutes until the vegetables are tender.

4   If the liquid seems rather thin, just mash some of the vegetables with a potato masher and stir to amalgamate. Taste and season if necessary, then stir in the coriander leaves just before serving.

SERVES 4

Tarragon potatoes with red onions, shallots and dolcelatte

This dish looks very pretty made with really tiny red onions – about 2 cm in diameter – if you can find them. I would also recommend the potato varieties *Pink Fir Apple* or *Ratte* here, given a choice, and have suggested you include torpedo-shaped shallots (*longues*). These make a nice visual contrast to the onions and potatoes, but of course any small shallots would be fine. A word of warning – if you want to make more than the amount below don't increase the vegetable stock in direct proportion to everything else or you'll end up with too much liquid.

- 220 g small red onions, evenly matched for size
- 220 g torpedo-shaped shallots, about the same size as the onions
- 450 g baby new potatoes
- 1 tablespoon olive oil
- 15 g butter
- 250 ml vegetable stock
- 2 tablespoons chopped tarragon
- 200 g dolcelatte cheese

1 If the onions or shallots seem particularly hard to peel, blanch them in boiling water for 1–2 minutes then drain, which will loosen the skins. Peel them but leave them whole unless they are large, in which case cut them lengthwise into manageable segments. If you need to cut them up try leaving some of the base attached – it stops them falling apart during cooking. Wash the potatoes, leaving them whole if they are small, otherwise cut them in half lengthwise.

2 Warm the olive oil and butter in a heavy, shallow frying pan (about 25 cm diameter), then fry the onions and shallots over a moderate heat until just starting to brown. Add the potatoes and continue frying for a few minutes, shaking the pan occasionally to turn the vegetables and stop them from sticking.

3 Pour in the vegetable stock and bring the contents of the pan to the boil. Turn the heat down, cover with a lid and simmer gently for 30–35 minutes until the vegetables are tender. Check near the end of the cooking time and, if much liquid remains, turn up the heat slightly, remove the lid and cook for a while, until the liquid is reduced to a few spoonfuls of thick sauce. Take the pan off the heat.

4 Add the fresh tarragon, stir well to mix, then drop chunks of dolcelatte over the surface of the vegetables. Put the lid back on for a couple of minutes until the cheese has melted.

SERVES 2

Slow-cooked potatoes with pasta, red onions and cream cheese

I have recently become intrigued by recipes that combine two or more different carbohydrate sources. The idea may seem odd, but is generally very successful. I remember being given hot mashed potato sandwiches as a child, so the idea is evidently not new. Here the potatoes are teamed with pasta, and the textures make an excellent combination. The preserved lemon adds a subtle tang and the whole is lubricated by a coating of hot melted cream cheese, flecked with Parmesan. Cold-weather comfort food of the first order.

- 1 tablespoon olive oil
- 15 g butter
- 220 g red onions, peeled and sliced
- leaves from 2 branches of fresh rosemary, stripped from the woody parts
- 450 g potatoes, peeled and cut into 2 cm dice
- ⅛ preserved lemon (page 198), finely chopped

- 300 ml vegetable stock
- 90 g pasta spirals or shells
- 150 g cream cheese
- a few tablespoons of milk
- salt and freshly ground black pepper
- 30 g freshly grated Parmesan cheese

Heat the olive oil and butter gently in a large heavy frying pan (about 30 cm diameter) and fry the onions and rosemary, stirring occasionally for 4–5 minutes, until the onion has started to soften. Add the potatoes and preserved lemon, stir and cook for a moment or two, then pour in the stock. Put the lid on the pan, turn the heat down and simmer gently for about 20 minutes, stirring occasionally, until the potatoes are tender.

Meanwhile boil the pasta in salted water until *al dente*, then drain and refresh it in cold water (this stops it sticking together). Put it to drain in a colander.

When the potatoes are done take the lid off the frying pan, stir the drained pasta into the potatoes and re-heat briefly. If more than a few tablespoons of stock remain, turn the heat up slightly and cook uncovered for a few minutes to drive off some steam. Pre-heat the grill.

Dilute the cream cheese with a small amount of milk to get a thick pouring consistency. Season the cheese with salt and freshly ground black pepper, then pour it over the potatoes and pasta mixture in the pan. There won't be enough to make a complete layer, so just distribute it around fairly evenly. Sprinkle with Parmesan and put the pan under the hot grill for a few minutes until the top is browned and bubbling.

SERVES 3

Baby onions and broad beans in a hot and sour tamarind sauce

This is a good dish for those times when you crave some big flavours. It has everything – hot, sweet and sour. Scotch Bonnet chillies (aka Habaneros) are generally very hot indeed, but the flavour they impart is incomparable. In the recipe below I've erred on the side of caution, so if you enjoy very spicy food you may want to increase the chilli.

- 15 g dried tamarind paste from a block
- 250 g small onions or shallots
- 2 tablespoons olive oil
- 1 medium onion, peeled and chopped
- 1 teaspoon black mustard seeds
- 1 teaspoon fennel seeds
- 1 teaspoon cumin seeds
- 3 or 4 cloves garlic, peeled and finely chopped
- 250 g broad beans, prepared weight (you will need about 500 g fresh beans in their pods to yield this amount, or use frozen)
- ¼ fresh Scotch Bonnet chilli, de-seeded and finely chopped (wear rubber gloves when handling and don't rub your eyes!)
- 2 teaspoons palm sugar

1 Chop the dry tamarind into small pieces, then pour on 3–4 tablespoons hot water. Stir well, pressing down on the tamarind with the back of a spoon to extract the flavour. Leave it to soak for a few minutes, then sieve the liquid, pressing as much as possible through the sieve but leaving behind the seeds and fibres. Set aside the tamarind liquid for later.

2 Blanch the small onions in boiling water to loosen their skins, then peel, leaving them whole. Heat the olive oil in a wide pan, large enough to hold the onions in one layer, and fry them briskly, shaking the pan from time to time for a few minutes until they go quite brown.

3 Temporarily remove the whole onions to a plate and add the chopped onion to the pan, turn the heat down a bit and fry for several minutes until the onion starts to soften. Add the mustard, fennel and cumin seeds, turn the heat up again and fry briskly for a moment or two, until they start to crackle. It's possible that you might need a touch more oil at this point. Add the garlic, broad beans, partly cooked whole onions and fresh chilli and stir well to combine.

4 Pour in the tamarind liquid and add the palm sugar and enough hot water to come about half way up the vegetables, then cover and simmer for about 30 minutes, stirring occasionally, until both beans and onions are tender. If there's much liquid left at the end, remove the lid, turn up the heat and allow most of it to cook off until just a few spoonfuls of concentrated, aromatic sauce remain.

SERVES 2

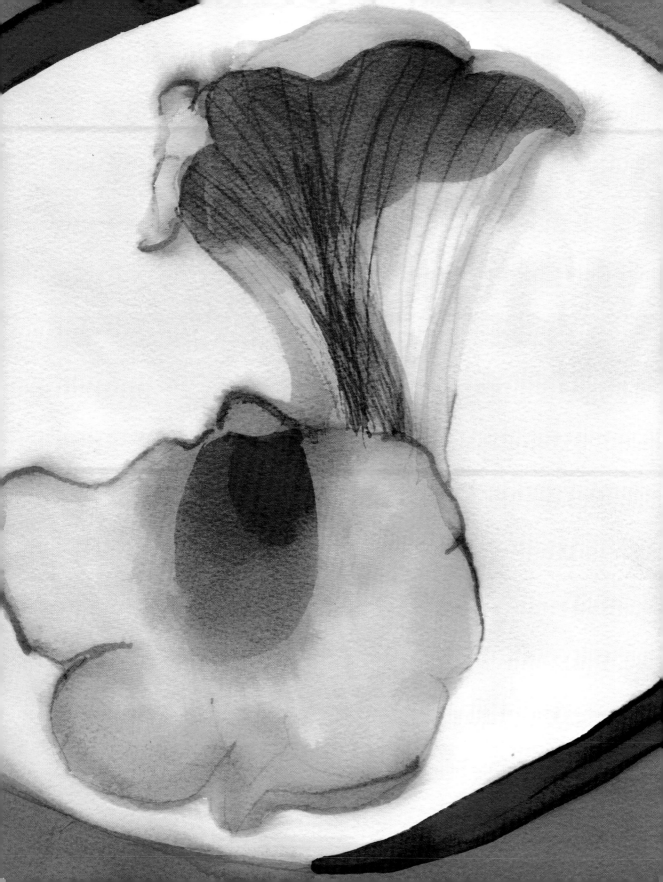

Wild mushroom and potato gratin with lemon salsa verde

A creamy and soothing gratin, jazzed up with a lively lemon salsa verde – a happy combination, and cold-weather comfort food *par excellence*. Some years ago I attended a weekend fungus foray course and learned how to identify wild mushrooms safely. It was great fun – I'd recommend it unreservedly – but don't pick wild mushrooms for the table unless you're 100% confident that you know what you're doing!

THE GRATIN

- 12 stalks fresh thyme leaves
- 1 small onion, peeled and left whole
- 2 bay leaves
- 150 ml milk
- 150 ml double cream
- salt and pepper
- 15 g butter
- 300 g mixed wild or exotic mushrooms, cleaned and cut into generous chunks
- 2 cloves garlic, peeled and thinly sliced
- 500 g floury potatoes, peeled and cut evenly into 3 mm slices

THE LEMON SALSA VERDE

- a handful parsley leaves
- 20–30 fresh mint leaves
- 1 clove garlic, peeled and crushed
- the finely grated zest and juice of 1 large lemon
- 1 rounded tablespoon capers, rinsed and drained
- 4 tablespoons olive oil
- salt and pepper

Oven temperature: 200°C (400°F, gas 6) – adjust for fan ovens

THE GRATIN

Put the thyme sprigs, onion, bay leaves, milk and cream in a small saucepan and heat gently to just below boiling point, season with salt and pepper, then cover the pan and set aside to infuse. Warm the butter in a wide shallow pan and fry the mushrooms over a moderate heat, stirring frequently, for about 10 minutes. Add the garlic for the last couple of minutes, making sure it does not burn, then set aside to cool for a few minutes. Soak the raw potato slices for 5–10 minutes in cold water to remove some of the starch, then drain them thoroughly in a colander.

In a shallow oven-proof gratin dish, 22 cm × 30 cm or equivalent, mix together the potato slices and the fried mushrooms. Separate the potato slices (using your fingers if necessary) as they have a tendency to stick together. Season with a little salt and pepper, bearing in mind you've already seasoned the liquid. Spread the vegetables quite evenly, then pour the cream infusion over them, fishing out the onion and bay leaves but leaving in the thyme. Gently press the potatoes under the liquid with the back of a spoon if necessary. Cover the dish and let it sit for about 20–30 minutes, allowing the flavours to mingle.

3 Bake, covered, in a pre-heated oven for about 45–60 minutes, until the potatoes are tender when tested with the point of a knife. Take off the lid, baste with the cooking liquid and bake for a further 10 minutes or so, until the top is golden brown.

THE LEMON SALSA VERDE

4 Whiz the parsley, mint leaves, garlic, lemon zest and capers in a food processor. Pour the olive oil, followed by the lemon juice, in a slow stream through the spout with the motor running. Stop the machine if necessary and scrape down the sides. Add salt and pepper to taste, and perhaps extra lemon juice. The sauce should be quite zingy to cut through the creaminess of the rich gratin. Serve the gratin with the sauce on the side.

SERVES 2–3

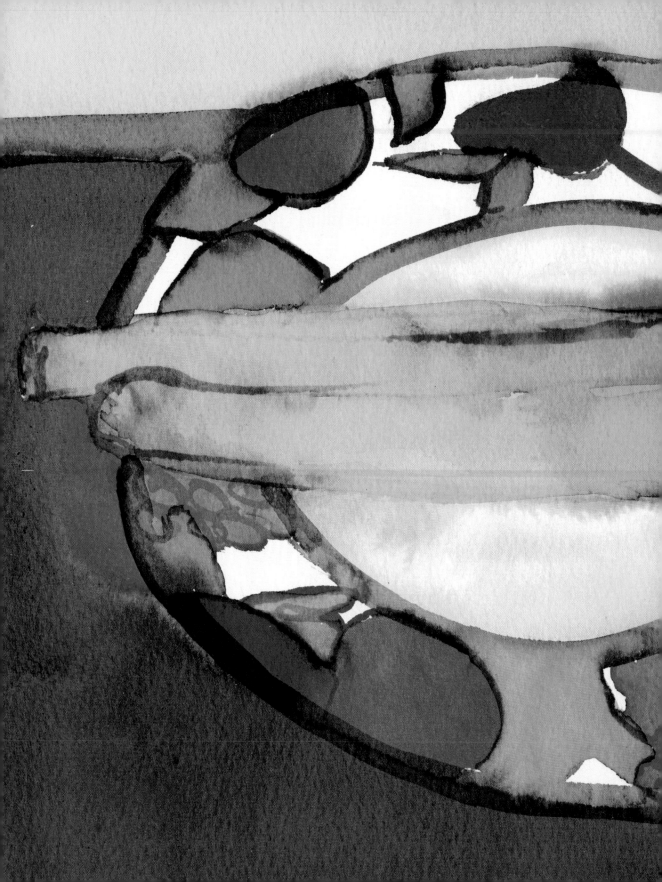

Leek, pasta and potato gratin with pecans and sage

Here is a useful cold-weather supper dish, which can be prepared in advance if necessary. It is quite rich so keep the accompaniments simple – some crisp salad would be sufficient. To roast pecan nuts pre-heat the oven to 180°C (350°F, gas 4) – adjust for fan ovens. Spread out the nuts in a single layer on a baking tray and cook for 10–14 minutes. Use a timer, as they burn very easily.

- 500 g new potatoes, scrubbed and diced
- 100 g dry pasta spirals or shells
- 15 g butter
- 1 kg leeks, cleaned, most of green part removed and cut into 1 cm rings
- 8–12 fresh sage leaves, chopped
- salt and pepper

- 170 g Gorgonzola cheese, de-rinded and cubed
- 40 g fresh grated Parmesan cheese
- 3 tablespoons double cream
- 30 g roasted pecan nuts, coarsely chopped
- freshly grated nutmeg
- 2–3 teaspoons fresh lemon juice

Oven temperature: 220°C (425°F, gas 7) – adjust for fan ovens

1 Simmer the potatoes in salted water until just tender (10–14 minutes, depending on their size and variety), then drain them thoroughly. Boil the pasta in salted water until just tender, then drain that, too.

2 Melt the butter in a wide, shallow pan and allow it to brown slightly over a moderate heat, then fry the prepared leeks for a couple of minutes, add the chopped sage and a little salt, cover the pan and cook gently for about 10 minutes until the leeks are tender.

3 Combine the leeks, potatoes and pasta and stir in the cubed Gorgonzola, grated Parmesan, cream and pecan nuts. Add a generous grating of nutmeg, plenty of freshly ground black pepper and salt if necessary. Taste, then stir in just enough fresh lemon juice to liven up the seasoning. Turn the mixture into a large oven-proof gratin dish, about 26 cm diameter. At this point you can cool the food, refrigerate it and cook it later or the next day, should you wish.

4 If baking it from cold, bring the dish to room temperature and bake for 20 minutes covered, then 10 minutes uncovered (30 in total). If the ingredients are still hot from preparation bake for 15 minutes covered and 5 minutes uncovered (20 in total).

SERVES 4

Potato and smoked garlic gratin with mixed greens and Brie

This recipe makes use of a particularly adaptable mixed salad sold pre-packed and ready-washed by various supermarkets. Spinach, watercress and rocket, delicious in the raw, also make for a peppery, savoury blend when cooked. You could vary the cheese to suit your own preferences so long as you choose one that melts well, such as dolcelatte or Taleggio.

- 200 g mixed spinach, rocket and watercress leaves
- 500 g waxy salad potatoes, washed and cut into 3 mm slices
- 1 tablespoon olive oil
- 40 g butter
- 2 small onions, peeled and sliced
- 3 fat cloves smoked garlic, peeled and sliced
- leaves from two 10 cm stalks rosemary, chopped
- salt and pepper
- 100 ml milk
- 150 g ripe Brie, or other good melting cheese (see above)

Oven temperature: 220°C (425°F, gas 7) – adjust for fan ovens

1 Bring a large pan of salted water to the boil and throw in the spinach, rocket and watercress mixture. As soon as the water comes back to the boil scoop out the wilted leaves with a slotted spoon and put them in a colander. Immerse the colander briefly in a bowl of cold water to stop the cooking process and set the colour, then put on one side to drain.

2 Using the same pan of boiling water simmer the potato slices gently for 4–6 minutes until cooked but not disintegrating, then drain and set them aside.

3 Warm the olive oil and two thirds of the butter in a wide, shallow pan and fry the onions until they are tender and beginning to brown (probably 10–15 minutes depending on the onions), then add the garlic and rosemary and fry for a couple of minutes more.

4 Take the pan off the heat and gently stir in the drained potato slices. Season with salt and pepper. Spread about half the potato and onion mixture in the bottom of a 19 cm diameter oven-proof gratin dish with sides at least 6 cm high, or equivalent.

5 Gently squeeze out the surplus water from the cooked greens, season them with a little salt and pepper and distribute them evenly over the potatoes. Dot with the remaining butter and arrange the remaining potato mixture in a layer on top of the greens.

6 Heat the milk until boiling, then pour it over the gratin. Dot the surface with chunks of Brie, cover the dish with a lid or foil and bake for about 20 minutes. Remove the lid and bake for a further 10 minutes to brown the surface.

SERVES 2–3

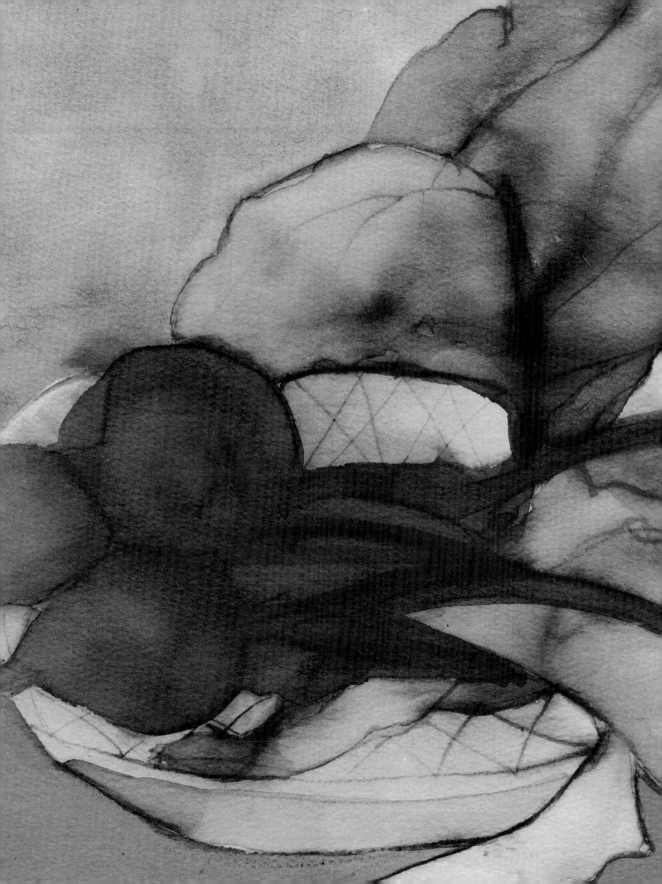

Beetroot and potato gratin with feta garlic cream

If your experience of beetroot is confined to the sad and soggy slices sold pre-cooked in nasty vinegar, allow me to put in a plea for the real thing, which is far superior. Why not try this – an interesting gratin that can be made any time from summer through to spring? It is best suited to cold-weather dining and is virtually a meal in itself. It looks dramatic, too, like stained glass windows on a plate. You could serve it with a dark green salad on the side – an arresting colour combination!

- 300 g beetroot, uncooked
- 500 g small salad potatoes
- 4 or 5 cloves garlic
- 1 thin slice fresh bread
- 60 g fresh Parmesan, grated
- 200 g Greek feta cheese

- 100 ml crème fraîche
- 60 ml milk
- about 10 g fresh dill leaves
- salt and pepper
- freshly grated nutmeg

Oven temperature: 200°C (400°F, gas 6) – adjust for fan ovens

You need a very wide, shallow gratin dish, about 30 cm diameter or equivalent, to make this recipe.

1 Prepare and cook the beetroot as described in the recipe for *Beetroot and potato tart with horseradish and Roquefort* on page 48. The cooking can be carried out in advance if more convenient. Drain the beetroot and, when cool enough to handle, peel and cut into wedges about the size of an orange segment.

2 Scrub the potatoes but leave the skin on, then cut them into wedges lengthwise, to match the beetroot. Simmer them with the un-peeled garlic cloves gently in salted water for about 8 minutes until just tender, then drain them and fish out the garlic.

3 Put the bread, broken up a little, and the Parmesan cheese in a food processor and whiz until they are reduced to fine crumbs, then tip onto a plate and set aside for later. Squeeze the garlic out of its skin and place the cooked cloves in the food processor. Add the crumbled feta, crème fraîche, milk and dill leaves to the bowl and whiz to a smooth paste. Season to taste with salt, pepper and grated nutmeg. You won't need much salt, given the saltiness of feta.

4 Arrange the potatoes and beetroot in a single layer in a wide gratin dish and pour the creamy sauce over them. Sprinkle on the breadcrumb mixture and cook in a pre-heated oven until the top is brown and crisp and the sauce is bubbling quietly – about 15–20 minutes.

SERVES 3

Wine-cooked celeriac and potato gratin with Emmental

I'm a big fan of celeriac, although my efforts at growing it have to date been spectacularly unsuccessful. It needs more consistent and regular watering than I manage to provide, so alas it's usually shop-bought for me! The main thing to remember about celeriac is that it discolours rapidly when peeled, so work fast and drop the slices into a bowl of cold water as you cut them.

- 1 tablespoon olive oil
- 15 g (½ oz) butter
- 2 medium-sized red onions, peeled and thinly sliced
- 450 g potatoes cut into 5–7 mm slices (peeled or not, as you prefer)
- 1 large celeriac, peeled, quartered and cut into slices the same thickness as the potatoes

- 1 teaspoon fennel seeds
- salt and pepper
- 170 ml white Bordeaux or other decent dry white wine
- 170 ml vegetable stock
- 150 g Emmental cheese, sliced
- 50 g fresh Parmesan cheese, grated

You will need a large frying pan, at least 28 cm diameter, with a well-fitting lid.

1 Warm the oil and butter together in the frying pan. Fry the onions, potato, celeriac and fennel seeds together for a few minutes, turning them over gently to make sure they are well mixed and not stuck together.

2 Add a generous grinding of black pepper, the wine and stock and bring the contents of the pan to the boil. Only add salt at this stage if your vegetable stock is home-made and you know it's not very salty, otherwise wait until later. Cook gently with the lid on the pan for about 25 minutes until the spuds and celeriac are tender, then check for seasoning, adding extra salt if needed.

3 Before doing anything else, pre-heat the grill. Remove the pan lid and cook down the liquid if much remains until you are left with a flavourful, concentrated few spoonfuls – enough to coat but not swamp the vegetables. Top with the cheeses and grill until brown and bubbling.

SERVES 4

Soufflé gratin

This dish is a hybrid – frittata meets soufflé. I wanted something eggy but light, with vegetables, too, and this was the result. The recipe below is the latest in a series of incarnations. I've tried it with several different cheeses and in the end concluded it needed something quite assertive, such as feta, to make its presence felt against the creamy richness of the eggs.

In this version I have used red peppers and red onions, but other vegetables would also enjoy this treatment. I quite fancy trying it with potatoes and as-paragus, or perhaps just leeks. . .

- 2 red peppers, de-seeded, de-veined and cut into bite-sized chunks
- 1 small red onion, peeled and chopped
- 1 tablespoon olive oil
- 15 g butter
- 2 cloves garlic, peeled and chopped

- 4 eggs, separated
- 100 g Greek feta
- 3–4 tablespoons double cream
- salt and pepper
- 2 tablespoons snipped chives
- 50 g finely grated Parmesan cheese

Oven temperature: 180°C (350°F, gas 4) – adjust for fan ovens

1 I make this dish in a large cast-iron frying pan with a detachable handle. If you don't have a similarly oven-proof frying pan, you will need to decant from the pan in which you cook the vegetables to a very wide, shallow oven-proof dish 30 cm diameter. In that case you need to warm the empty dish by putting it in the hot oven for at least 5 minutes, otherwise the timings given will be way out.

2 In a wide, shallow pan, fry the peppers and onions in the olive oil and butter quite briskly for about 5 minutes until they start to brown, then turn the heat right down, put a lid on the pan and cook gently, stirring from time to time, for about 30 minutes until the peppers are perfectly tender. Add the garlic to the pan for the last 2–3 minutes of cooking time so that it softens without burning.

3 While the vegetables are cooking whiz the egg yolks, feta cheese, cream, salt and pepper to a smooth paste in a food processor. Stir in the chives and about half the Parmesan, saving the rest for later. Whisk the egg whites until stiff and snowy, then gently fold in the yolk mixture.

4 Decant the cooked vegetables to the pre-heated oven-proof dish if necessary, then pour the egg mixture around the cooked vegetables. Sprinkle the remain-ing Parmesan over the surface and cook in a pre-heated oven, middle shelf or above, until just set (10–15 minutes).

SERVES 2–3

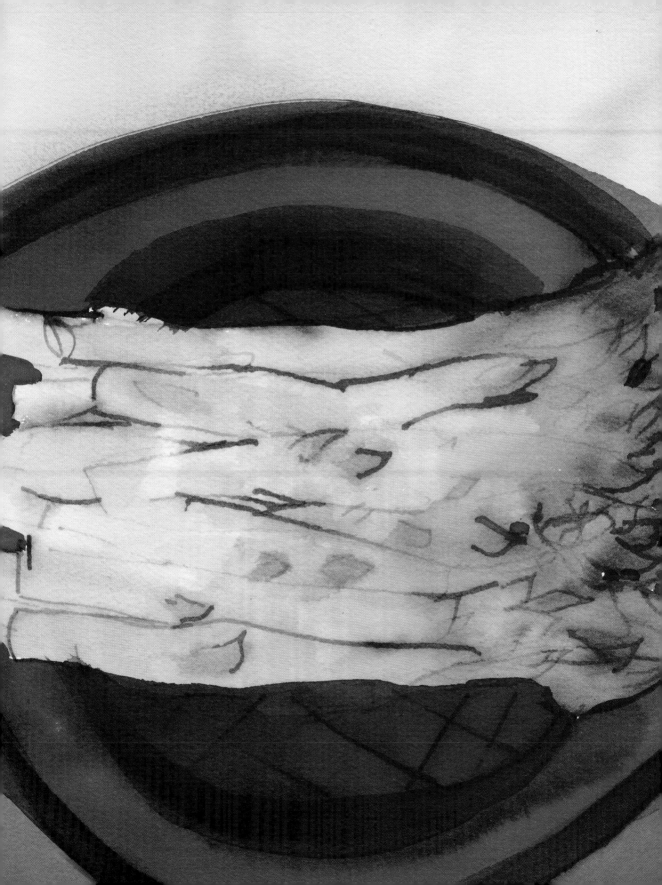

Asparagus and potato frittata

This is a bright but delicate spring frittata, bursting with vitality. The asparagus season is short but sweet, rather like spring itself. It seems to start quite slowly, but before you know it the spears are springing up thick and fast, burgeoning before your eyes. From a gardener's point of view asparagus requires patience and forward planning – you can't start to harvest it until three years after planting. The prospect of this long, frustrating wait led me to plant not one but three asparagus beds, so now, for about six weeks a year, we're swimming in the stuff!

- 250 g new potatoes, scrubbed and cut into even chunks if large, otherwise left whole
- 250 g fresh asparagus
- 6 eggs
- 1 tablespoon olive oil
- 15 g butter
- 150 g Greek feta cheese, coarsely crumbled
- about 10 g (2 tablespoons) chopped fresh mint

Simmer the new potatoes in salted water until tender, then drain and cut them into 1 cm dice. While the potatoes are cooking prepare the asparagus by trimming off and discarding the tough bottom part of the spears. You can easily tell where the spears start to toughen – just flex each spear very gently in your hands. Towards the tip they will feel quite bendy. The further down the spear you go, the stiffer they get, and towards the bottom they feel very rigid. Chop them off where stiff meets bendy, and peel if the skin seems at all tough.

Cut the prepared asparagus into 2 cm sections, keeping the tips separate. Steam the lower sections for about 7 minutes or until tender, adding the tips to the steamer after 2 minutes (they take less time to cook). These times are very approximate since asparagus is infinitely variable, so start testing early.

Beat the eggs with a fork just enough to amalgamate them, then season with salt and pepper. Heat the olive oil and butter in a large, heavy frying pan (28–30 cm diameter), until the butter foams and the pan is quite hot. Pour in the eggs (the pan should be hot enough to make them sizzle) and immediately turn down the heat to quite low. The idea is to set just the bottom of the frittata so, unless you're using a gas hob, you may need to take the pan off the heat for a few moments so the rest of it doesn't cook too quickly.

Swiftly scatter the cooked asparagus and potatoes into the frittata and cook gently for 10–15 minutes or until the base is set but the top still looks quite moist. About half way through this period pre-heat the grill.

Scatter the crumbled cheese evenly over the surface of the frittata and slide the pan under the hot grill for a couple of minutes to set the top. Sprinkle with the chopped mint just before serving. Serve hot or, better still, lukewarm with some decent bread and a big, leafy salad.

SERVES 2–3

Chard frittata with feta, mint and preserved lemon

Cooking can sometimes be rather like gardening, in that the best combinations are often accidental. The first time I made this frittata I had intended to use tarragon and parsley but, having also chopped fresh mint and chives for a potato salad, I put those in by mistake! The result was delicious so I decided to keep it that way. The tarragon and parsley were quite good in the potato salad, too, and no-one else was any the wiser. . .

This recipe specifies a large quantity of chard – home-grown amounts rather than shop-bought. You could get away with using half quantity, if the cost seems prohibitive. Although the recipe calls for leaves only, don't bin the stalks. They will keep in the fridge (well wrapped) for a couple of days and are good added to a stir-fry or soup. Although I've included this recipe with main course dishes this frittata makes excellent picnic food. It has a robust flavour that stands up to outdoor dining and is sturdy enough to be quite portable.

- 15 g butter
- 1 tablespoon olive oil
- 2 onions, peeled and chopped
- 3 cloves garlic, peeled and finely chopped
- $\frac{1}{8}$ preserved lemon, finely chopped (recipe on page 198 or use a chunk of scrubbed fresh lemon)
- about 800 g chard leaves, stalks removed (but see above), washed, dried in a salad spinner and coarsely chopped
- 2 tablespoons chopped fresh mint
- 2 tablespoons chopped fresh chives
- 8 eggs, lightly beaten and seasoned with salt and pepper
- 200 g Greek feta cheese, coarsely crumbled

1 This is quite a hefty frittata and calls for a large frying pan about 30 cm diameter. Heat the butter and olive oil in the pan and fry the onions until they are quite soft and starting to go brown. Add the garlic and preserved lemon and cook for a couple of minutes, followed by the chard leaves. Stir for a few minutes more over a moderate heat until the leaves start to wilt.

2 Stir about two thirds of the chopped mint and chives into the beaten eggs, reserving the rest for later. Spread the vegetables evenly over the base of the pan and pour in the seasoned beaten eggs, then turn the heat down quite low and cook gently without stirring for 10–15 minutes, until the base of the frittata is set but the top is still quite runny. A couple of minutes before you think this point will be reached, pre-heat the grill.

3 Scatter the crumbled feta cheese evenly over the frittata and finish under the hot grill, cooking it just until the top is set. Let the frittata cool for about 10 minutes and scatter over the remaining green herbs just before serving.

SERVES 3–4

Tomato and pepper frittata

In its first incarnation this was a late summer dish using garden produce. I used to avoid green peppers, believing that the riper red ones always had more flavour, but my home-grown peppers ran out of summer in which to ripen and I had to do something with them. I was pleasantly surprised by the outcome, to the extent that I now regularly buy green peppers out of season in order to make this.

- 450 g ripe tomatoes, peeled and coarsely chopped
- salt and pepper
- 1 tablespoon olive oil
- 15 g butter
- 300 g green peppers, cut into large chunks
- 6 eggs
- 15 g shredded basil leaves
- 170 g Greek feta cheese, cubed

1 Cook the tomatoes briskly in a large (30 cm diameter) heavy frying pan, shaking the pan occasionally, until their liquid has all but evaporated – at this point they should be chunks rather than soup. Transfer them to a bowl for later.

2 Rinse and dry the frying pan, then warm the oil and butter in it over a gentle heat until the butter has melted and starts to foam. Fry the green peppers over a gentle heat for 20–30 minutes until they are completely tender, stirring frequently.

3 Meanwhile beat the eggs in a bowl just enough to combine the yolks and whites and season well with salt and pepper.

4 Before doing anything else put the grill on to heat. Pour the beaten eggs into the pan with the peppers and give it a swirl. Dot the tomato chunks over the surface of the egg and leave the pan alone for about 3 minutes, until the frittata starts to set underneath. The top should still be quite runny.

5 Distribute the shredded basil and feta chunks evenly over the frittata and put the pan under the pre-heated grill for a couple of minutes until the top is just set.

SERVES 3 AS A MAIN COURSE, 6 AS A STARTER

Green risotto with fresh peas and mint cream

Rice and peas are a classic Italian combination, here made more lively still by the addition of mint and lemon zest. This is a very quick and straightforward recipe, particularly if you use frozen peas!

- 1 tablespoon olive oil
- 15 g butter
- 1 large onion, peeled and finely chopped
- grated zest from 1 lemon
- 110 g Arborio or other risotto rice
- 170 ml dry white wine
- 2 rounded teaspoons Marigold Swiss Vegetable Bouillon powder
- 300 g petits pois, fresh or frozen (weight after shelling)
- about 15 g fresh mint leaves
- salt and pepper
- 4 tablespoons cream
- fresh grated Parmesan cheese to serve

1. Warm the olive oil and butter together in a wide, heavy pan and fry the chopped onion and lemon zest for a few minutes, until the onion begins to soften. Add the rice and give it a good stir, then pour in the wine and put a timer on for 15 minutes. Let the wine bubble and reduce for a few minutes, while you bring a kettle of water to the boil.

2. Add the bouillon powder to the pan and a good slug of boiling water from the kettle, enough to just submerge the rice. Let the risotto simmer away, stirring and adding boiling water from the kettle from time to time when the rice seems in danger of drying out. Add the peas to the pan 15 minutes after the wine was added to the rice and bring the contents back to a simmer. Cook for a further 5 minutes or thereabouts.

3. The rice will be done about 20 minutes from the time when liquid is first added, in this case the wine, and you should ensure that when this point is reached there is not much liquid remaining.

4. Meanwhile, between stirrings, place the washed and dried mint leaves in a pestle and mortar and pound them to a paste with a pinch of salt. Stir the cream into the mint paste to make a smooth, pale green sauce.

5. When the rice and peas are cooked taste the risotto and season if necessary. You probably won't need much salt as the bouillon powder is quite salty, but pepper might be a good idea. Stir a little fresh grated Parmesan cheese into the risotto and serve each portion with a little mint cream poured over.

SERVES 2

Mushroom and durum wheat risotto

A fairly new grain product has recently arrived on the supermarket shelves. *Ebly* is perhaps the most common brand name for partially-cooked whole durum wheat grains – the type of wheat often used to make pasta. You cook it in water or stock for 15–20 minutes, and it retains its shape, has a pleasant flavour and a satisfyingly chewy texture. Here it forms the basis for an excellent 'risotto' that does not require much stirring.

This recipe calls for roasted pine kernels. Roasting nuts really intensifies their flavour and is well worth the effort. To roast pine kernels pre-heat the oven to 180°C (350°F, gas 4) – adjust for fan ovens. Spread out the kernels in a single layer on a baking tray and cook for 5–7 minutes until they have turned a rich golden-brown colour. Use a timer, as they burn very easily.

- 10 g dried mushrooms, preferably ceps
- 150 ml boiling water
- 15 g butter
- 1 tablespoon olive oil
- 1 large or 2 small onions, peeled and chopped
- ¼ preserved lemon (page 198), finely chopped (use a piece of fresh lemon, rind included, if you don't have any preserved)
- 200 g fresh mushrooms, cleaned and coarsely chopped
- 150 g durum wheat such as *Ebly*
- 1 teaspoon Marigold Swiss Vegetable Bouillon powder
- salt and pepper
- 15 g bunch flat-leaved parsley, finely chopped
- 30–60 g roasted pine kernels
- fresh grated Parmesan cheese to serve

1   Soak the dried mushrooms in the measured boiling water for 20 minutes, then drain them off through a fine sieve, saving the soaking water. Rinse the mushrooms under running water to remove any grit or dust, then chop them finely.

2   Heat the butter and olive oil together in a wide, shallow pan and fry the soaked, dried mushrooms, chopped onion and lemon for a few minutes. Add the fresh chopped mushrooms and fry for about 3–4 minutes more.

3   Add the Ebly, stir to coat, then pour in the reserved mushroom-soaking water. Stir in the bouillon powder, cover the pan and simmer gently for 15–20 minutes until the wheat is cooked to your liking and all the liquid is absorbed. Depending on the ferocity of your stove, the thickness of your pan and so on, you may need to stir occasionally or top up with a little extra hot water during the cooking time.

4   Taste and add salt and pepper if necessary, then stir in the parsley and roasted pine kernels just before serving. Serve with fresh grated Parmesan cheese.

SERVES 2

Oriental egg fried rice

This savoury fried rice is a meal in itself and also makes a good accompaniment to stir-fried vegetables.

- 110 g Thai fragrant rice
- salt
- 1 tablespoon groundnut oil
- 1 small onion, peeled and chopped
- 2 stalks of celery, cut into diagonal slices 3 mm thick
- 2 cm cube ginger, peeled and thinly sliced
- 2 cloves of garlic, peeled and sliced
- 1 fresh red chilli pepper, de-seeded and finely chopped
- 2 eggs, beaten
- 2–3 tablespoons chopped fresh coriander leaves
- soy sauce to serve

1 Put the rice to soak in plenty of cold water for at least 30 minutes, then drain and rinse it thoroughly. Put it in a saucepan with a heavy base and a well-fitting lid, then add 170 ml of cold water and ½ teaspoon of salt. Bring it up to the boil, then reduce the heat as low as it will go – use a heat-diffuser if you have one – the rice should be barely simmering. Put the lid on the pan and, after 10 minutes, stir the rice gently with a fork, then cover again and cook for another 10 minutes (20 minutes in total). By now the rice should have absorbed all the water and be completely tender.

2 While the rice is cooking, heat the oil in a frying pan and fry the onions, celery and ginger, adding a little salt, over a medium heat, stirring frequently for 10–15 minutes until quite tender. Add the garlic and chilli and cook for about 3 minutes more, then turn off the heat and set aside for later.

3 When the rice is done, put the sautéed vegetables back over a gentle heat and pour in the beaten egg. Stir gently with a fork until the egg is scrambled, then add the cooked rice, stir with the fork to amalgamate and just heat it through for 2–3 minutes. Taste and add extra salt if needed, then stir in the coriander leaves and serve immediately.

4 Put soy sauce on the table when you serve this but don't add any during cooking as it spoils the colour.

SERVES 2

Lemon and basil couscous with mushrooms and tomatoes

This dish makes a lovely, light and fresh-tasting supper. Finish the vegetable preparation before you start to cook – once underway the dish is ready very quickly.

To roast pine kernels pre-heat the oven to 180°C (350°F, gas 4) – adjust for fan ovens. Spread out the kernels in a single layer on a baking tray and cook for 5–7 minutes. Use a timer, as they burn very easily.

- 1 large onion, peeled and chopped
- 2 tablespoons olive oil
- 30 g butter
- 2 cloves of garlic, crushed
- ⅛ preserved lemon (page 198), finely chopped – use a chunk of un-peeled fresh lemon if you don't have any preserved
- 250 g couscous
- 400 ml well-flavoured vegetable stock
- 250 g mushrooms, cleaned and quartered
- 1 large, ripe tomato, cut into chunks
- salt and freshly ground black pepper
- 10 basil leaves, shredded
- 1 tablespoon roasted pine kernels
- fresh grated Parmesan cheese

You need a pan with a well-fitting lid for this recipe.

1 Sauté the onion in 1 tablespoon olive oil and half the butter over a medium heat until softened and slightly browned. Add the garlic, just for the last couple of minutes of the onion cooking time to avoid burning it, then stir in the preserved lemon and couscous.

2 Pour in the hot vegetable stock and stir gently with a fork to break up the lumps of couscous, then cover the pan, turn the heat down as low as it will go and cook very, very gently for about 15 minutes. If the base of your pan is rather thin or your heat at all fierce use a heat diffuser.

3 While the couscous is cooking, fry the chopped mushroom in 1 tablespoon olive oil and the remaining butter over a moderate heat for about 12 minutes, adding the tomato chunks for the last 3–4 minutes of cooking time. If you heat the tomatoes without actually cooking them, they keep their lovely fresh flavour.

4 Taste the couscous for seasoning and add salt if necessary, then gently fork in the shredded basil, breaking up any lumps in the couscous as you do so. Stir the mushrooms and tomatoes gently into the couscous, add a scattering of pine nuts and top with a little fresh Parmesan.

SERVES 2

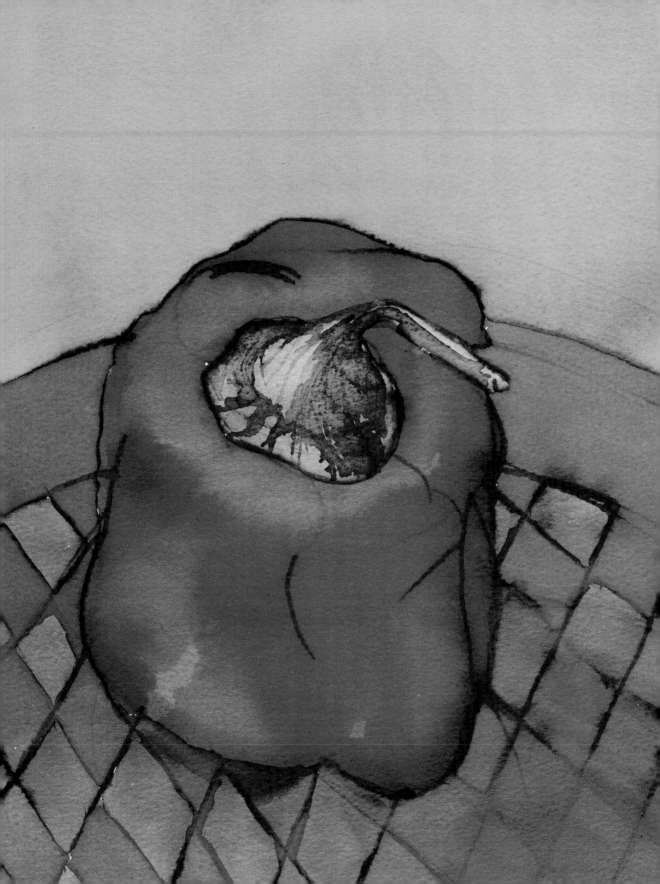

Roasted red pepper couscous with mint, feta and lime

Not all red peppers are the same. Wonderful heirloom varieties exist, some with a very distinctive paprika flavour, but unfortunately they're not widely available in the shops. This simple supper dish has a good combination of textures and flavours and will taste delicious made with standard supermarket ingredients. It's sensational with sun-ripened peppers of a tasty variety, but you'll probably have to grow them yourself. It's worth a go – even without a greenhouse – so long as you live in one of the warmer counties and have a sheltered section of south-facing wall against which to ripen them.

- 2 or 3 ripe red peppers, de-seeded and cut into hefty chunks
- 2 cloves garlic, peeled and crushed
- 3 tablespoons olive oil
- a pinch or two of sea salt
- about 6 spring onions, very thinly sliced – keep the green parts separate
- 15 g butter
- 170 g couscous
- 260 ml vegetable stock
- about 15 g fresh mint leaves, chopped
- 200 g Greek feta cheese, diced
- 1 tablespoon balsamic vinegar
- 8–12 black olives, preferably Kalamata
- 2 chunky wedges of lime

Oven temperature: 230°C (450°F, gas 8) – adjust for fan ovens

1 Toss the pepper chunks with one of the crushed garlic cloves and 2 tablespoons of the olive oil in a wide baking dish. Sprinkle with a little salt and roast them in a pre-heated oven for about 30 minutes, turning them over after about 20 minutes. Keep an eye on them for the last 10 minutes of the cooking time to make sure they don't burn.

2 About 10 minutes after the peppers have gone into the oven get the couscous underway. Fry the white parts of the spring onion and the rest of the crushed garlic in a mixture of 1 tablespoon of olive oil and the butter. After a couple of minutes add the couscous and stir. Pour in the vegetable stock, bring it to the boil, then turn the heat right down as low as it will go, cover the pan and cook without disturbing it for 15 minutes, by which time the peppers should be about ready.

3 To assemble the meal, fork the raw, green spring onion and half the chopped mint gently into the couscous. Place the hot, cooked red peppers and their juices in a bowl with the cubed feta, the rest of the mint and the balsamic vinegar, and toss together. Add the black olives, stir and serve the mixture on top of the hot couscous, giving each diner a generous wedge of lime on the side.

SERVES 2

Spinach and durum wheat risotto

Here is another recipe using the type of durum wheat described on page 78. This 'risotto' is a gentle, soothing mixture of flavours. Any tannin in the spinach is subdued by the addition of modest amounts of butter and cream.

Although flecked with scarlet chilli, this recipe is not especially fiery since a very mild chilli is used, just enough to give a slight kick. The supermarkets have recently been selling some beautiful, fresh slender red chillies about 8 cm long that look like mini versions of Romano peppers. They are mild (by most chilli standards) and make a terrific addition to many dishes. If you can be bothered to slice them into thin rings and pick out the seeds they make a pretty garnish. Of course if the prospect of any chilli at all is too much to contemplate just leave it out, the dish will still taste fine.

- 15 g butter
- 1 tablespoon olive oil
- 1 large or 2 small onions, peeled and chopped
- 2 cloves garlic, peeled and crushed
- 1 red chilli, de-seeded and finely chopped (cut a few rings to garnish)
- 150 g durum wheat such as *Ebly*
- 230 ml vegetable stock
- 2–300 g fresh spinach leaves, washed, well drained and cut into 1 cm ribbons
- freshly grated nutmeg
- salt and pepper
- 2–3 tablespoons cream (optional)
- 30–60 g fresh Parmesan cheese, grated or shaved

1. Heat the butter and olive oil in a wide pan, then fry the chopped onions over a moderate heat until softened and slightly browned. With my home-grown onions this takes only 5–10 minutes, but shop-bought onions may take quite a bit longer.

2. Add the garlic and chopped chilli (leave the chilli rings for later), followed by the durum wheat. Give the pan a stir and pour on the vegetable stock. Cover and simmer for 15 minutes.

3. Add the spinach and cook, stirring gently, for 3–5 minutes until the spinach is just tender. Add a generous grating of nutmeg and season to taste with salt and pepper.

4. Stir in the cream, if using it, and serve topped with the Parmesan cheese and a few red chilli rings.

SERVES 2

VARIATION – SPINACH AND WHEAT WITH GORGONZOLA

Omit the cream and Parmesan cheese from the recipe. At the end of the cooking time dot some generous chunks of Gorgonzola cheese (150 g is about right for this quantity) evenly over the surface of the risotto and put the lid back on the pan for 2–3 minutes until the cheese has melted.

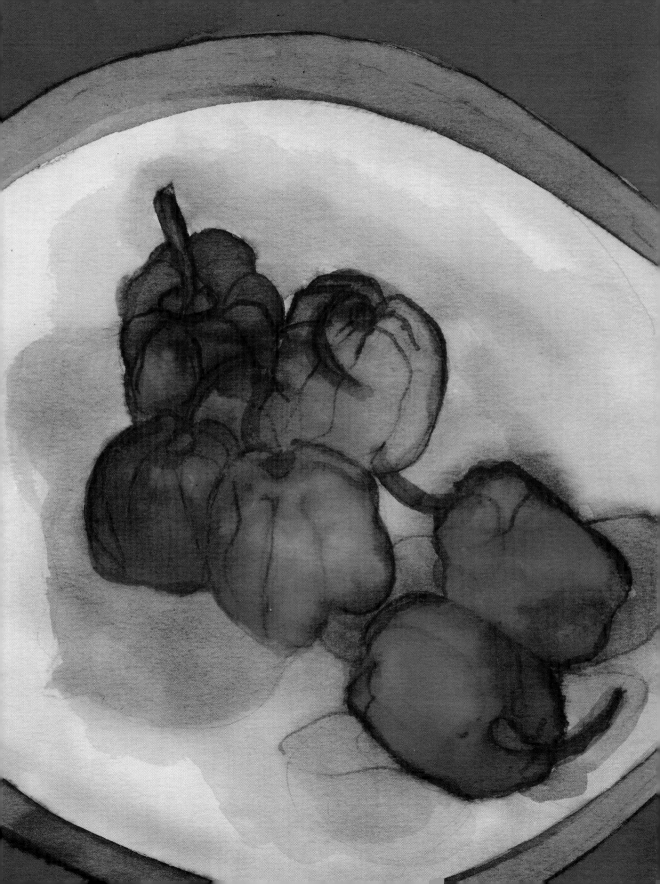

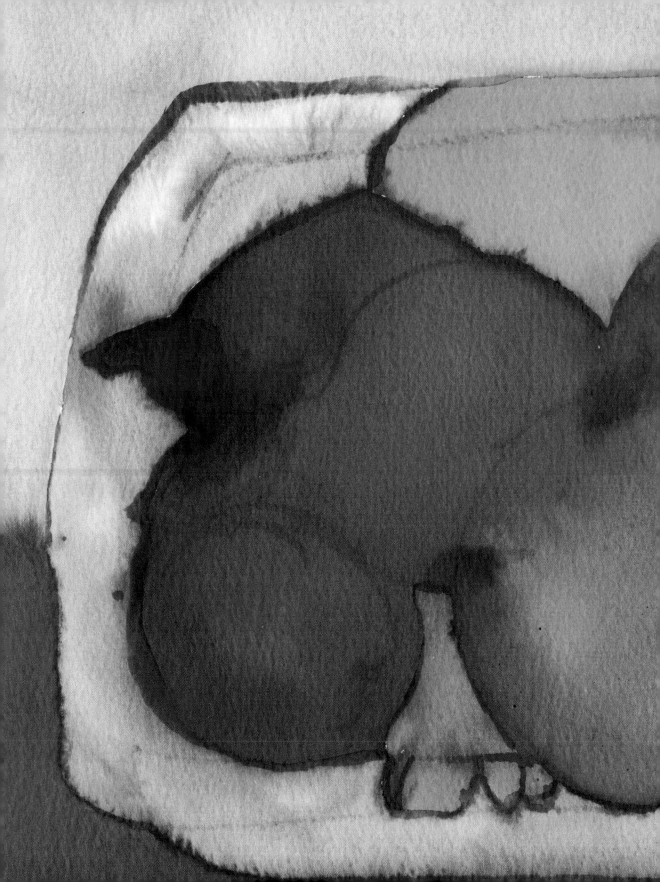

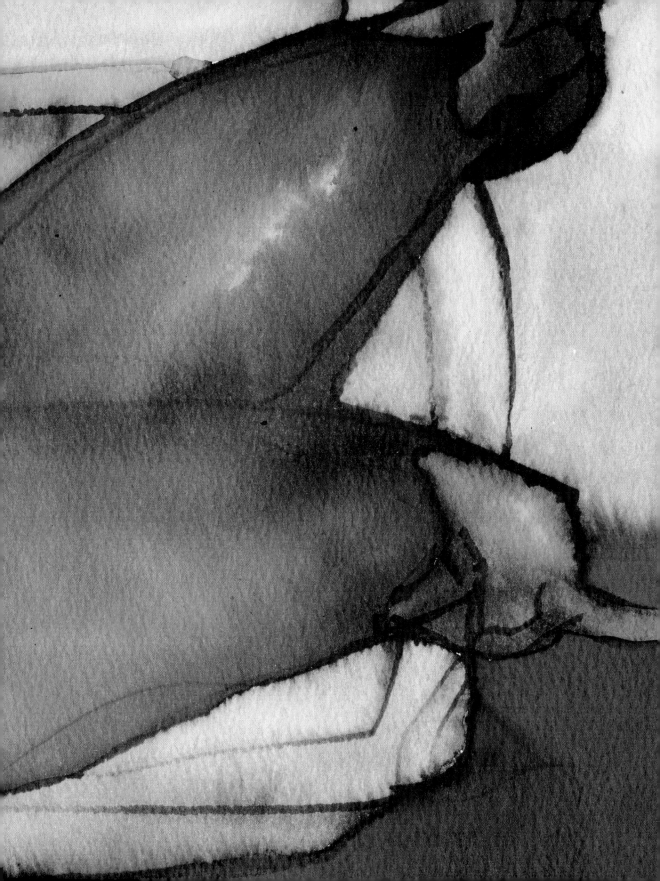

Garlic-spiked aubergines with a crisp croustade, with Lebanese parsley sauce

A simple and savoury meal with a distinctly Middle-Eastern flavour, this recipe uses less oil than many similar aubergine dishes. Serve the aubergines with the sauce on the side, accompanied by a crisp salad and any of the potato dishes from the *Companion Dishes* chapter. The hot, crispy aubergines also make a terrific sandwich filling! Try them in warm pitta bread with lots of crunchy salad and some garlic mayonnaise.

THE AUBERGINES

- 3 medium aubergines
- salt and pepper
- 6 cloves garlic, peeled and cut into thin slivers
- 4–5 tablespoons olive oil
- 1 slice good bread, white or wholewheat
- 50 g fresh Parmesan cheese, roughly diced
- 50 g sesame seeds

THE SAUCE

- 3 tablespoons tahini
- 3 tablespoons fresh lemon juice
- 15 g parsley leaves, washed and the thickest stalks removed
- 1 clove garlic, peeled and crushed
- salt to taste, about ½ teaspoon
- 1 tablespoon olive oil

Oven temperature: 200°C (400°F, gas 6) – adjust for fan ovens

You will need an oven-proof dish big enough to hold six aubergine halves in a single layer.

THE AUBERGINES

1. Cut the aubergines in half lengthwise and sprinkle the cut surfaces with salt, then place them in a colander for about 30 minutes to degorge. Rinse them thoroughly under running water and pat dry with kitchen paper.

2. Using a small, sharp knife, make a cross-hatched pattern of deep slits in the aubergine flesh, being careful not to cut all the way through. Push slivers of garlic into these slits, sharing the garlic evenly between the aubergines. Season the cut surface of the aubergines with salt and pepper. Put about a tablespoon of olive oil in the baking dish and spread it evenly over the base. Pack the aubergine halves into the dish cut side up, and drizzle or brush them with more olive oil – about 2 tablespoons – then cook uncovered in a pre-heated oven, middle shelf or above, for about 45 minutes until quite tender.

3. While the aubergines are in the oven make the croustade. Break up the bread and put it and the Parmesan chunks in a food processor, season with salt and a good grind of black pepper, and add 1–2 tablespoons olive oil. Whiz until reduced to fine crumbs, then mix in the sesame seeds.

4 Remove the partially cooked aubergines from the oven and gently press down
on the flesh with the back of a tablespoon to flatten them and close up the slits.
Share out the croustade mix between them, pressing it down with the back of
a spoon. Return them to the oven and cook for a further 15–20 minutes, or
until the aubergines are tender and the croustade is crisp and golden-brown.

THE SAUCE

5 Put all the sauce ingredients in a food processor bowl and whiz until the sauce
is smooth and the parsley finely chopped. You will need to add a few tablespoons of boiling water through the processor spout while the machine is
running, to thin the mixture. The sauce should have the consistency of pouring
cream. Taste and add salt at the end until it is to your liking.

SERVES 3

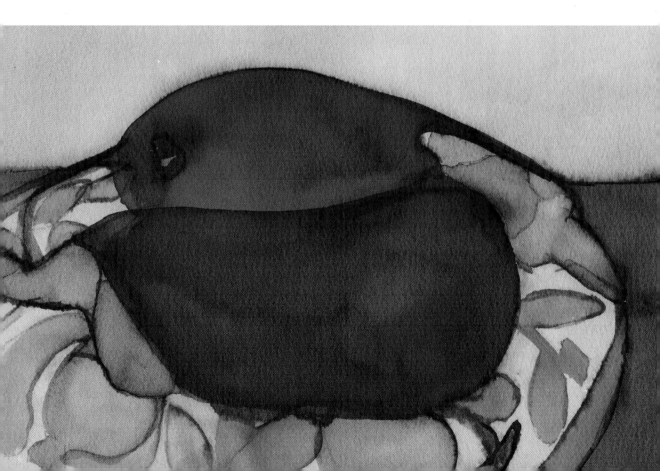

Twice-cooked onions stuffed with mushrooms and wild rice

This is a tasty and versatile recipe that could fill different roles – starter or main course – the choice is yours. For a main course allow two per person. I think it's worth roasting the pine kernels for this recipe – it definitely brings out the flavour. Pre-heat the oven to 180°C (350°F, gas 4) – adjust for fan ovens. Spread out the kernels in a single layer on a baking tray and cook for 5–7 minutes. Use a timer, as they burn very easily.

- 6 large onions, about 10 cm diameter
- 1 teaspoon Marigold Swiss Vegetable Bouillon powder
- 100 g wild rice
- 30 g butter
- 250 g mushrooms, cleaned and quartered
- 2 cloves garlic, peeled and finely chopped
- 1 fresh red chilli, de-seeded and finely chopped
- 30 g roasted pine nuts
- 2–3 tablespoons finely chopped parsley leaves
- finely grated zest from 1 lemon, plus some of its juice
- salt and pepper to taste
- sesame oil and soy sauce to serve

Oven temperature: 200°C (400°F, gas 6) – adjust for fan ovens

1   Peel the onions, leaving them whole, then simmer in salted water for 15 minutes. Rinse in cold water, then carefully remove the middles, leaving a shell no more than 3 onion layers thick. Use the discarded centres in some other dish such as a soup.

2   Bring a pan of water to the boil, add a teaspoon of Marigold bouillon powder and simmer the rice for about 50 minutes, until tender. Drain thoroughly and set aside for later.

3   Heat about half the butter in a wide shallow pan and fry the mushrooms quite briskly, stirring frequently for 10–15 minutes, until they are well cooked and have lost much of their water content. Add the garlic and chilli for the last couple of minutes, being careful not to let them burn.

4   Take the pan off the heat and stir in the pine nuts, parsley, lemon zest and cooked rice. Taste and season with salt and pepper and some of the lemon juice as necessary. I like the filling to be quite tangy, you may prefer it less so. You may also want to add more chopped chilli at this stage.

5   Fill the hollowed out onions with the stuffing mix, melt the remaining butter, brush it over the onions and bake, uncovered, in a pre-heated oven, middle shelf, for about 30 minutes. Drizzle the onions with a spoonful or two of sesame oil and a little soy sauce before serving.

SERVES 3 AS A MAIN COURSE, 6 AS A STARTER

Stilton soufflé-filled baby pumpkins

This recipe is lovely so long as you have well-flavoured pumpkins or squash. It was devised to use autumn-ripening pumpkins rather than their more insipid summer relations. I find the lower fat crème fraîche works better here than the really solid type but, if the latter is what you have, dilute it with a little yogurt or milk. Although I've included this with main course dishes it also makes a good starter.

- 3 grapefruit-sized small pumpkins or squash
- about 15 g butter, melted
- salt and pepper
- 240 g Stilton cheese (rind removed), cut into chunks
- 200 g crème fraîche, preferably less than full fat
- 2 eggs, separated
- 6 hefty stalks of parsley
- 6 small spring onions, finely sliced, including some green
- 60 g walnuts, coarsely chopped
- a generous squeeze of fresh lemon juice

Oven temperature: 220°C (425°F, gas 7) – adjust for fan ovens

You will need a large baking dish or roasting tin big enough to hold the pumpkin halves in a single layer.

1 Cut the little pumpkins in half, top to bottom, then scoop out and discard the seeds. Take a thin slice off the outside of each pumpkin half so they will sit without wobbling. Prick their insides with a fork, being careful not to puncture them.

2 Brush the pumpkin shells inside and out with the melted butter. Season them with salt and pepper, put them in the baking dish and cook in a pre-heated oven for about 15 minutes or until they are tender. The time this takes can vary quite a lot, depending on the pumpkin variety.

3 While the pumpkins are cooking make the filling. Whiz together the Stilton, crème fraîche, egg yolks and parsley leaves in a food processor. You can mix the ingredients by hand if necessary, but you will need to chop the parsley very finely.

4 Whisk the egg whites in a very large, clean, dry bowl until they form stiff white peaks. Push them gently to one side, then slide the cheese and egg yolk mixture down the other side of the bowl to avoid deflating the whites. Fold the egg whites gently into the cheese mixture.

5 Gently fold in the spring onions and walnuts, then season to taste with pepper and lemon juice. You probably won't need salt as Stilton is usually very salty. Spoon the filling into the pre-cooked pumpkin shells and return them to the oven for about another 10 minutes, until the filling is risen and a golden brown colour on top.

SERVES 3 AS A MAIN DISH, 6 AS A STARTER

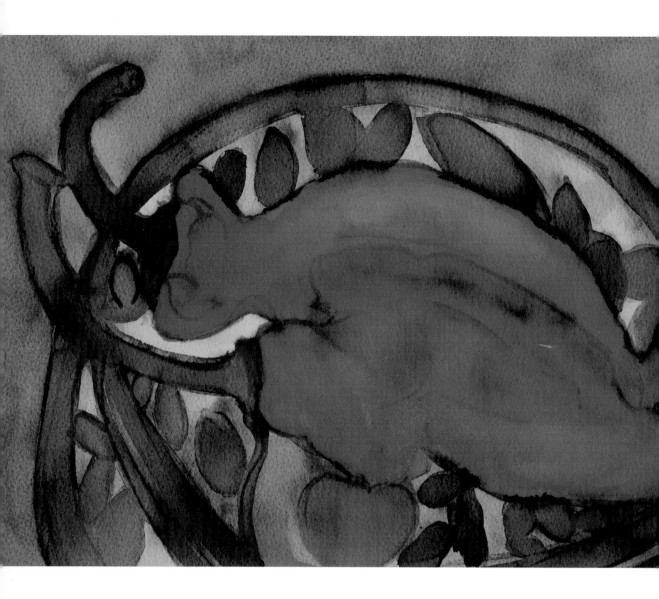

Romano peppers stuffed with feta, pine kernels, mint and lemon

Romanos (sometimes called *Ramiros*) are long, pointed, red or yellow sweet peppers, which have thinner walls and usually a sweeter flavour than ordinary bell peppers. They look very elegant and would be good served with potatoes and a crisp salad.

- 2 Romano peppers
- 1 large onion, peeled and chopped
- 15 g butter
- 1 tablespoon olive oil
- 1 clove garlic, peeled and finely chopped
- 200 g Greek feta cheese, drained, rinsed, dried and crumbled

- ¼ preserved lemon, finely chopped (page 198)
- 4 tablespoons fresh mint leaves, chopped (about 15 g)
- 50 g pine kernels (preferably roasted)
- freshly ground black pepper

Oven temperature: 200°C (400°F, gas 6) – adjust for fan ovens

1 Cut the peppers in half lengthwise, leaving the stalks attached, remove the seeds, then rinse and dry the pepper halves.

2 Fry the onion in the butter and olive oil over a moderate heat until tender. Add the garlic to the pan and cook for a couple of minutes longer, then set the pan aside to cool slightly.

3 Whiz the feta, lemon and mint to a smoothish purée in a food processor, stopping the motor and scraping the mixture down from the sides as necessary. Put the cheese purée and pine kernels into the pan with the fried onions and mix thoroughly, taste and adjust the seasoning. You will certainly need black pepper but the mixture may be salty enough due to the presence of feta.

4 When you're happy with it, pile the mixture into the pepper halves and place them in an oiled baking dish. Cover the dish with foil or a lid and cook in a pre-heated oven for 30 minutes, then remove the lid and bake uncovered for a further 10–15 minutes, until the surface of the filling is browned and bubbling.

SERVES 2

Baked celeriac mash topped with poached eggs

A delicious and savoury winter dinner, this is virtually a meal in itself, needing only a crisp, green salad on the side.

- 450 g floury potatoes, peeled and diced
- 1 medium celeriac root, peeled and diced
- 1 medium onion, peeled and chopped
- 15 g butter
- 1 tablespoon olive oil
- 2 cloves garlic, peeled and crushed
- 2–3 tablespoons finely chopped parsley
- about 90 ml cream
- salt and pepper
- 3 large eggs
- a few shavings of fresh Parmesan cheese

Oven temperature: 200°C (400°F, gas 6) – adjust for fan ovens

1   Boil the potatoes and celeriac separately in salted water until both are tender, then drain. While they are cooking, fry the onion in the butter and olive oil over a moderate heat until tender and starting to brown, adding the garlic for the last couple of minutes of cooking time. Set aside for later.

2   Mash the potatoes or put them through a potato ricer. Purée the celeriac thoroughly in a food processor until smooth. Don't be tempted to put the spuds in the food processor – it makes them go glutinous. Combine the potatoes and celeriac, then stir in the parsley, fried onions and about three quarters of the cream. Season to taste with salt and pepper.

3   Share out the mixture between three oven-proof individual bowls about 16–18 cm in diameter, level the surface and make an egg-sized hollow in each portion using the back of a spoon. Run a fork over the surface so you'll get brown, crispy ridges. Bake for 20–25 minutes until they start to brown.

4   Poach the eggs about 7 minutes before the bases will be ready. I use an egg poacher pan with lift-out cups, but I know many people prefer to cook them directly in boiling water. When their whites are set but the yolks still runny, put the eggs into the celeriac hollows. Pour the reserved cream over them, scatter on some Parmesan shavings and a grinding of black pepper and return the bowls to the hot oven for a couple of minutes to melt the cheese.

SERVES 3

Roast leeks with mint and feta

This is another savoury winter supper dish that is mercifully fast and simple to put together. It needs a carbohydrate-laden companion dish such as *Slow-cooked potatoes in brown butter with red onions, rosemary and Reblochon* (page 119) or just plain baked potatoes, unless you're dieting!

- 1 kg leeks (weight before preparation), trimmed, washed and cut in half lengthways
- 1–2 tablespoons olive oil
- 1 teaspoon rock salt
- 200 ml dry white wine
- 200 g Greek feta cheese, cut into 1 cm dice
- 15 g finely chopped fresh mint
- 30 g fresh grated Parmesan cheese

Oven temperature: 220°C (425°F, gas 7) – adjust for fan ovens

1 Lay the leeks in an oven-proof dish and brush them with olive oil. Sprinkle on the rock salt and pour the wine into the bottom of the dish. Cover the dish with foil (or a lid) and cook for 40 minutes in total.

2 Keep covered for the first 20 minutes, then uncover and dot with the cubed feta which has been tossed with the chopped fresh mint and Parmesan cheese. Cook for another 20 minutes.

SERVES 3

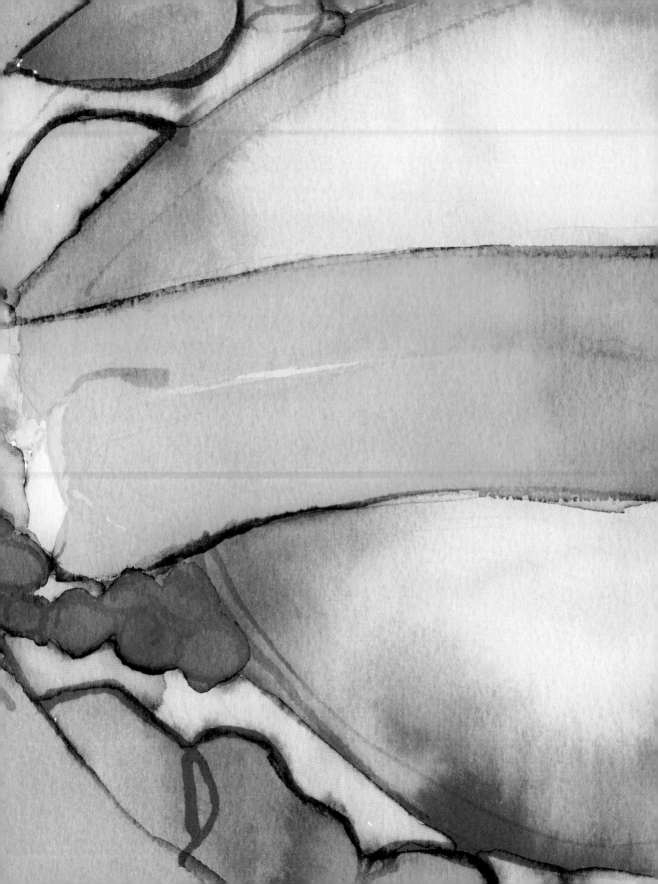

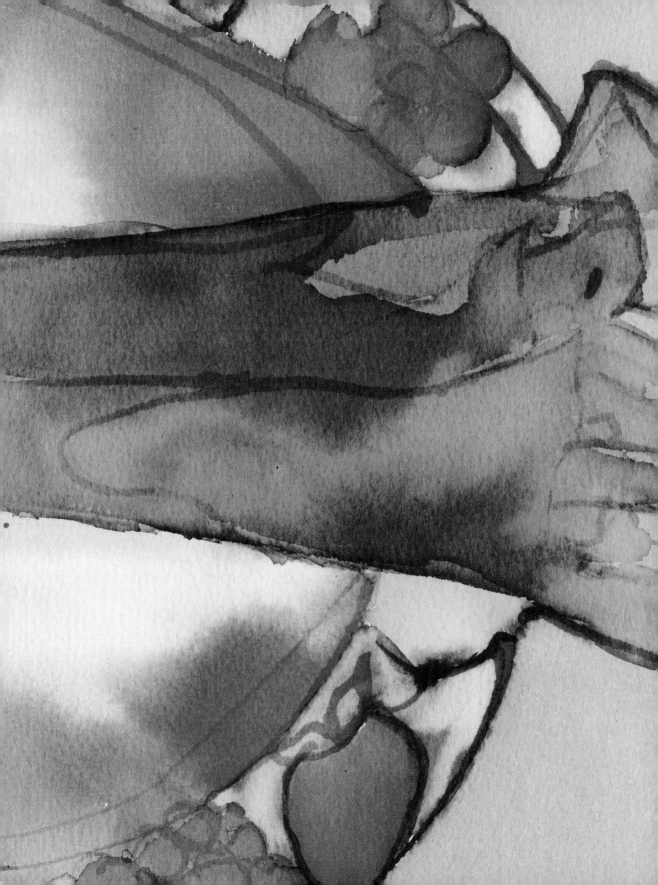

Spinach and pumpkin sauce for gnocchi

This pumpkin and spinach sauce for gnocchi looks glorious on the plate, with its lively colour scheme of orange and green. I suggest you use a packet of fresh gnocchi from the deli or supermarket chill counter. The quality is pretty good and, although gnocchi are quite straightforward to make from scratch, the process is fairly laborious. The dish makes a warming autumn or winter meal and the sauce is also suitable for pasta.

Choose a reliably well-flavoured squash such as butternut or better still grow your own, which will give you a much wider choice of variety than you get in the greengrocers. Squash are also a lot of fun to have in the garden. Dramatically fast-growing, they make excellent starter plants to get children interested in raising food. If you only grow one variety I recommend 'Turks Turban' for its excellent flavour, vigour of growth and completely outrageous appearance.

- 1 pumpkin or squash weighing about 500 g, de-seeded, peeled and cut into 1 cm dice (weight before preparation)
- 15 g butter
- 1 tablespoon olive oil
- ½ teaspoon salt
- 4 cloves garlic, peeled and crushed
- about 200 g spinach leaves, cleaned, drained and coarsely shredded
- 500 g fresh gnocchi
- 100 g crème fraîche
- freshly ground black pepper
- fresh Parmesan to serve

1 Prepare the squash by first cutting it in half lengthwise with a big, sharp knife. Scoop out the seeds and fibres with a spoon and discard them. Now place the squash halves cut-side down and cut into slices 1 cm wide. Put each slice flat (cut side) on the chopping board and slice off the skin with a few swift downward strokes of the knife.

2 Warm the butter and olive oil in a heavy frying pan and add the salt. Fry the squash over a moderate heat for between 10 and 25 minutes, stirring frequently, until the chunks are slightly browned and quite soft. The cooking time for winter squash is very variable so test a piece from time to time.

3 Add the garlic and spinach to the pan and continue to cook for a further 2–3 minutes, stirring, until the spinach wilts and the squash is completely tender. Meanwhile cook the gnocchi according to the instructions on the packet.

4 Just before serving, add the crème fraîche to the squash and spinach, plus a generous grinding of pepper. Stir in the cooked, drained gnocchi and serve in pre-warmed bowls, topped with freshly grated Parmesan cheese.

SERVES 2–3

Herbed pumpkin and pine nut sauce for pasta

This is a cheerful and savoury sauce for pasta. The flavour is quite delicate so use a higher sauce-to-pasta ratio than normal. The quantity below really is only enough for two or three, although it looks quite generous. Serve the sauce on plainly cooked pasta, gnocchi or even baked potatoes, and pass round extra Parmesan at the table.

The pine kernels add a welcome crunch. To roast pine kernels pre-heat the oven to 180°C (350°F, gas 4) – adjust for fan ovens. Spread out the kernels in a single layer on a baking tray and cook for 5–7 minutes. Use a timer, as they burn very easily. I usually roast a large batch then cool and store the surplus, as they're a useful item to have on hand.

- 250 g raw, diced pumpkin or winter squash (you'll need a squash weighing about 400 g to yield this amount of flesh)
- 15 g butter
- 1 tablespoon olive oil
- 2 onions, peeled and chopped
- 6 cloves of garlic, peeled and crushed
- 90 ml crème fraîche
- a few tablespoons of vegetable stock
- salt and pepper
- 60 g roasted pine kernels
- 2 tablespoons of finely-chopped parsley or chives
- fresh Parmesan cheese, grated

1 Steam the pumpkin over salted water until completely tender (immersion is anathema to pumpkins and destroys their delicate flavour). Test after about 7 minutes, but the cooking time can vary quite a bit. Purée in a food processor or just mash with a potato masher, as you prefer.

2 Melt the butter and oil in a wide, heavy saucepan and sauté the onions in it over a moderate heat, stirring frequently, until they are soft and beginning to go brown. Add the garlic, turn down the heat and cook for a few minutes longer.

3 Whisk the crème fraîche into the pumpkin purée and dilute with a little vegetable stock to the consistency of thick pouring cream. Pour this mixture into the pan with the onions, stir well, taste and add salt if necessary. Give the pan a generous grind of black pepper and heat the sauce gently without letting it boil. Just before serving stir in the pine kernels, fresh herbs and a little grated Parmesan.

SERVES 2–3

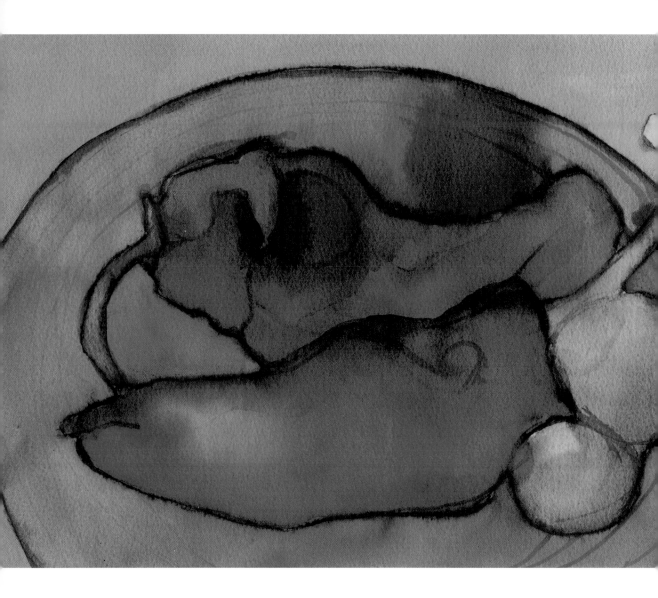

Red sauce for pasta

This is a recipe from Andrew, my husband. Fusion food in the extreme, it combines Mediterranean vegetables, Greek yogurt, Italian cheese, Franco-German wine and oriental chillies for good measure. I thought it sounded like a complete dog's breakfast when he reeled off the list of ingredients, but the proof of the pudding as they say... It was delicious, and I ate my critical words along with the pasta. Perhaps regional authenticity is a subject about which cookery writers tend to be too precious?

- 30–40 g roasted pine kernels
- 2 Romano or other red peppers, washed, de-seeded and chopped
- 1 large or 2 small red onions, peeled and chopped
- 1 large mild green chilli, de-seeded and finely chopped
- 3 cloves of garlic, peeled and finely chopped
- 15 g butter
- 1 tablespoon olive oil
- salt and pepper
- 1 glass (about 220 ml) Gewürztraminer
- 2 tablespoons Greek yogurt
- 2 tablespoons chopped fresh tarragon
- fresh grated Parmesan cheese to serve

1 To roast the pine kernels pre-heat the oven to 180°C (350°F, gas 4) – adjust for fan ovens. Spread out the kernels in a single layer on a baking tray and cook for 5–7 minutes. Use a timer, as they burn very easily.

2 Sauté the peppers, onions, chilli and garlic together for a few minutes in the oil and butter. Add about 1 teaspoon salt and the wine, then cook gently for about 30–40 minutes, until the vegetables are tender and the wine much reduced. Season to taste and stir in the yogurt, tarragon and pine nuts just before serving.

3 Serve the sauce on hot, plain pasta with a crisp side salad and pass around the Parmesan cheese and the leftover Gewürztraminer.

SERVES 2

Wild rocket and tomato sauce for pasta

If you can't get wild rocket, ordinary will be fine – when I concocted this sauce I just happened to have wild in the fridge. Whichever type you use, stir it into the sauce just before serving – it should be barely wilted when you eat it.

- 2 onions, peeled and chopped
- 1 tablespoon olive oil
- 2 cloves garlic, peeled and chopped
- 600 g fresh, ripe tomatoes, peeled and chopped
- 4 tablespoons cream or crème fraîche
- 100 g wild rocket, coarsely chopped
- salt and pepper
- you might also need lemon juice or white wine vinegar and a pinch of sugar
- fresh grated Parmesan cheese to serve

1 Fry the onions in the olive oil for a couple of minutes, then add the garlic and tomatoes and simmer over a gentle heat for about 40 minutes until the sauce has thickened. Stir in the cream or crème fraîche and rocket and cook for about 2 minutes, just until the rocket wilts. Season to taste with salt and pepper.

2 Taste and, if the sauce seems a bit lacking in zing, add a squeeze of fresh lemon juice or a small splash of white wine vinegar. If the tomatoes were less than perfect you may need a pinch of sugar, too.

3 Serve stirred into plain cooked pasta (500 g fresh pasta is about right for 4 people) and pass the Parmesan at the table.

SERVES 4 ON PASTA

COMPANION DISHES

Roast asparagus in lemon butter with pine kernels

Roast asparagus is very different to steamed or boiled. It's chunkier and more assertive, perhaps not how you'd like to eat it at the beginning of the season, but a welcome change when the initial novelty wears off. Although I've included it here with other companion dishes, this recipe would be equally at home as a starter.

- 20 g butter
- grated zest and juice of 1 lemon
- pinch of salt

- 500 g asparagus spears
- 20–30 g pine kernels

Oven temperature: 220°C (425°F, gas 7) – adjust for fan ovens

1 Trim the asparagus, removing the tough bottom section of the spears, as explained in the recipe for *Asparagus and potato frittata* (page 73). Peel the stalks, starting about 3 cm below the tips, using a potato peeler. This may seem rather a fiddle but if you don't do it the skins are likely to stay tough during roasting.

2 Place the butter, lemon zest and juice in a roasting tin and put it in a pre-heated oven until the butter has melted. Add a little salt and toss the asparagus spears in the lemony butter so they are well coated.

3 Cover the tin with foil or a lid and roast for 30 minutes. Remove the lid, scatter the asparagus with pine kernels and put it back in the oven uncovered for 5 minutes or until the pine kernels are golden brown.

SERVES 2

Stir-fried Savoy cabbage with chilli and ginger

A lively, spicy stir-fry for a winter day when you feel in need of a kick-start from something dark green and elementally healthy! If I've been over-indulging in the dairy department I'll sometimes eat this for dinner just with plain rice or noodles. It feels virtuous to eat without being bland, although you can of course tone down the chilli heat should you so desire. For a more orthodox meal, serve the cabbage with *Oriental egg fried rice* (page 80).

- 1 tablespoon groundnut, or other bland cooking oil
- 1 red onion, peeled and chopped
- 2 cm cube of fresh ginger, peeled and finely chopped
- 1 or 2 fresh red chillies (use more or less to taste), de-seeded and finely chopped
- 1 small Savoy cabbage, leaves finely shredded, washed and well drained
- natural soy sauce to taste

1 Heat the oil in a large saucepan or wok until sizzling, then add the onion. Stir-fry for 1 minute, then add the ginger and chillies. Stir-fry for 1 minute or less, then add the cabbage. Stir-fry over a medium heat for about 5 minutes until tender but still with some crunch.

2 If you feel the cabbage is in danger of burning before it is sufficiently cooked, turn the heat down much lower and cover the pan with a lid for a couple of minutes so it steams a little, then remove the lid and turn up the heat to finish. Season with natural soy sauce and serve immediately.

SERVES 2

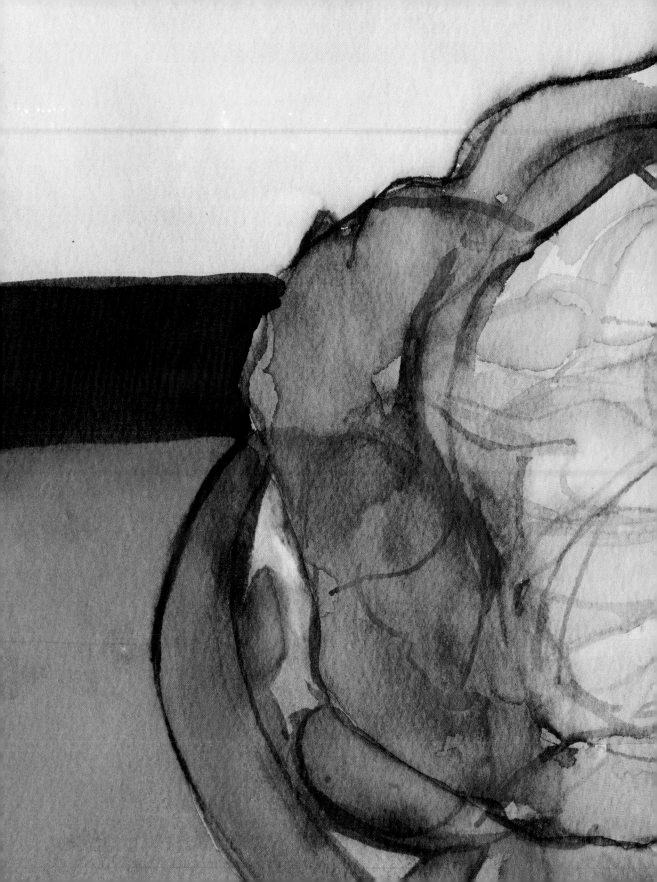

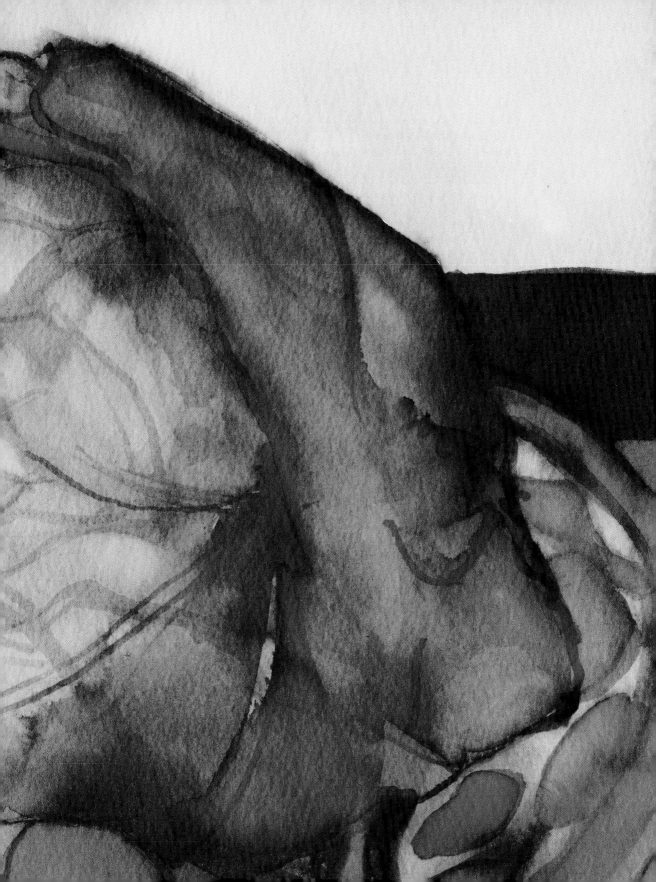

Garlic lovage mash

Lovage is a great favourite of mine. It has a strong, celery-like flavour and is a doddle to grow, although not always easy to find as a cut herb in the shops. If you can't get hold of it use parsley (or even tarragon) instead. It won't be the same but it'll still taste good.

- about 800 g floury potatoes, peeled and cut into even chunks
- 4 cloves garlic, peeled and crushed
- 1 tablespoon olive oil
- 30 g butter
- 100–150 ml milk
- 10–15 g fresh lovage leaves, washed, dried and finely chopped
- salt and pepper

1 Simmer the potatoes in salted water until tender. While they're cooking, gently fry the garlic in the olive oil for a few minutes.

2 Drain the potatoes, return them to the pan in which they were cooked and mash them with the butter and milk. Re-heat gently, add the fried garlic and chopped lovage to the mashed potatoes, stir well and adjust the seasoning to taste.

SERVES 4

Oven-baked potato cakes

I have loved Central-European potato cakes ever since a Jewish friend first cooked them for me more than twenty years ago. Traditionally they're fried so I rarely make them because, in common with many people, I try to avoid fried food. These oven-baked potato cakes are low in fat, without sacrificing the spirit of the original.

You might serve them with *Fried spinach and chickpeas with lovage and cream* (page 52) or any of the frittata recipes starting on page 73.

Grating onions can be painful on the eyes, so if you find yourself afflicted you might like to try my novel solution to this problem – swimming goggles! Don't let the neighbours see you though, or it won't be long before the men in white coats turn up.

- about 15 g butter for the baking trays
- 600 g potatoes, peeled and finely grated
- 1 small onion, peeled and finely grated
- 2 eggs, lightly beaten
- 1 level teaspoon salt

Oven temperature: 180°C (350°F, gas 4) – adjust for fan ovens

You will need a couple of large metal baking trays, generously buttered.

1 Grate the potatoes quite finely – a food processor with a grating attachment will speed things up. Take the grated potato a handful at a time and squeeze it as hard as you can, discarding the copious amounts of liquid that come out.

2 Mix the squeezed potatoes with the grated onion, beaten eggs and salt. Place heaped teaspoons of this mixture on the buttered baking trays, pressing down firmly with the back of a fork to make circular cakes, not more than 5 mm thick. Try to get the cakes quite thin at the edges, so they go crispy in the oven.

3 Bake the potato cakes in the middle of the oven for about 35 minutes in total, turning them over carefully with a thin spatula after 20 minutes, until they are golden brown and crisp around the edges.

SERVES 4

Baby aubergines baked with rosemary and lemon thyme

If, like me, you're susceptible to all things mini, you may already have been beguiled by those cute little packs of tiny aubergines to be found on the produce shelves of certain supermarkets. If so, here's something nice to do with them. These little aubergines would make a lovely accompaniment to a cheesy baked potato or, for something more refined, team them with *Tomato and pepper frittata* (page 76) and *Basil and pistachio bread* (page 177).

- 1 tablespoon olive oil
- 3 heaped teaspoons of sun-dried tomato paste
- 250 g baby aubergines, washed and halved lengthwise
- 2 red onions, peeled and cut into hefty chunks

- leaves from 3 sprigs rosemary
- leaves from a small bunch of lemon thyme
- salt and pepper
- 8 Kalamata olives, stoned

Oven temperature: 200°C (400°F, gas 6) – adjust for fan ovens

1 Mix together the olive oil and tomato paste, then thin to the consistency of single cream with a little hot water. Put the aubergines, onions, rosemary and thyme in a bowl, pour in the tomato-oil mixture and turn everything over a few times to coat thoroughly. Season with salt and pepper.

2 Place in a single layer in a shallow baking dish, cover with foil and bake for 40–50 minutes until the vegetables are tender. Remove the foil, dot with the olives and return the dish to the oven for about 5 minutes to dry out slightly. Adding the olives near the end of the cooking time retains their succulence.

SERVES 2

Potatoes with lovage and tarragon

Here is a simple but delicious variation on the classic *pommes boulangère* theme. Adaptable and very forgiving, it can be made in advance, re-heated and eaten at any temperature from lukewarm to piping hot, to suit whatever you're serving with it. It would go well with any of the frittatas or stuffed vegetables from the *Main Courses* chapter. Any of the more robust herbs such as sage, rosemary or thyme could be substituted for the lovage and tarragon but you'd need less of them (about half the amount given below) as they're stronger in flavour.

- 500 g small waxy salad potatoes, washed and cut into 3 mm slices
- 1 onion, finely chopped
- 1 level tablespoon finely chopped lovage
- 1 level tablespoon finely chopped tarragon
- 3 cloves garlic, peeled and cut into wafer-thin slices
- 10 g butter
- 1 level teaspoon Marigold Swiss Vegetable Bouillon powder
- salt and pepper

Oven temperature: 180°C (350°F, gas 4) – adjust for fan ovens

1 Put the potato slices, onion, lovage, tarragon and garlic in a large bowl and toss them together, much as you might do with a salad, to separate the potatoes and distribute the other ingredients evenly.

2 Put the butter and bouillon powder in a measuring jug and make up to 150 ml with hot water from the kettle. Add this liquid to the potatoes, season to taste and toss again.

3 Tip the mixture into a wide, shallow baking dish (24 cm × 20 cm × 3 cm or equivalent), cover with foil and bake for 30 minutes, then remove the foil and bake for a further 30 minutes until the top is starting to brown and the potatoes are tender.

SERVES 2–3

Roast caramelized butternut squash with tarragon

Roasted squash makes a good accompaniment to many autumn or winter main course dishes and can also form the basis for a soup, risotto or pasta meal in its own right. It is an ingredient in both *Spiced pumpkin dip* (page 20) and *Herbed pumpkin and pine nut sauce for pasta* (page 99). Roasting drives off much of the moisture and intensifies the flavour, and the addition of a small amount of sugar helps to bring out the natural sweetness of the squash.

- 15 g butter
- 2 tablespoons olive oil
- ¼ teaspoon brown sugar
- 1 butternut squash (22–25 cm long), halved, peeled, de-seeded and cut into 1 cm slices
- 1 heaped tablespoon chopped fresh tarragon
- salt and pepper

Oven temperature: 240°C (460°F, gas 8) – adjust for fan ovens

1 Put the butter into a large baking tin or dish – one which is big enough to hold the squash in a single layer. Place the tin in a pre-heated oven for a few minutes to melt the butter, then add the olive oil and sugar. Give it a stir and add the squash, turning the chunks so they are evenly coated in the oil and butter mixture. Add the tarragon, season to taste with salt and pepper and stir again.

2 Roast the squash uncovered in the hot oven for about 15 minutes, until it is tender and flecked with brown. There's no need to turn the chunks over so long as they are in a single layer.

SERVES 4 AS A SIDE DISH

Slow-cooked potatoes in brown butter with red onions, rosemary and Reblochon

This is the type of dish I make for supper when there's nothing to eat in the house apart from a few spuds and onions. It does, however, require some decent and quite strongly-flavoured cheese, of a type that will melt invitingly. The Reblochon is by no means compulsory. Substitute Taleggio, Brie, Gorgonzola, almost any kind of goat's cheese – whatever you fancy.

If you use floury potatoes the dish will disintegrate quite a bit, which is fine. Waxy spuds will hold their shape better and give a dish with a rather different character.

- 30 g butter
- 1 tablespoon olive oil
- 500 g potatoes, peeled and cut into bite-sized chunks
- 300 g red onions, peeled and roughly chopped
- leaves from three 12 cm sprigs fresh rosemary
- 4 large cloves garlic, peeled and chopped
- 250 ml vegetable stock
- about 200 g Petit Reblochon or other cheese (see above), cut into generous chunks

1 Warm the butter in a heavy frying pan until it starts to brown, then add the olive oil. Add the potatoes, onions and rosemary leaves to the pan and fry, stirring occasionally, for about 5 minutes.

2 Add the garlic and fry for another minute or so, then pour in the vegetable stock. Bring the contents of the pan to a simmer, put on a well-fitting lid and cook gently for 20–25 minutes, stirring once or twice to prevent sticking.

3 When all the vegetables are tender remove the lid and, if the dish seems at all watery, allow some of the liquid to cook off. Turn up the heat if necessary. When most of the liquid has gone dot the surface with chunks of cheese and put the pan under a pre-heated grill for a couple of minutes until the cheese is bubbling and flecked with brown.

SERVES 2–3

Slow-cooked potatoes with leeks, lemon thyme and mozzarella

As with some of the other potato dishes in this chapter, I was in a quandary about where to put this recipe. Although I've included it with companion dishes, I often treat it as a main course, served with a green or mixed salad on the side. I've made this dish with both old and new potatoes, with equal success. It's also quite good using Cheddar instead of mozzarella.

Lemon thyme is a lovely and reliable herb, both easy to grow and attractive to look at, and is productive even in the depths of winter when there is little else around in the way of garden aromatics. It isn't widely available in supermarkets but you are unlikely to experience difficulties finding a plant in the garden centre. It will adapt quite happily to life in a pot so long as you can give it a sunny spot and stop it from getting water-logged or frozen solid in the winter.

- 1 kg potatoes, scrubbed and cut into wafer-thin slices
- 4 medium-sized leeks, trimmed and cut into wafer-thin slices
- 2–3 tablespoons olive oil
- 2 tablespoons fresh lemon thyme leaves
- salt and pepper
- 200 g mozzarella cheese, sliced
- 50 g grated Parmesan

You will need a 30 cm lidded frying pan for this amount of vegetables. If you cook them in a smaller pan the timings will be way out.

1 Slice the potatoes and leeks as thinly and evenly as possible. Use a food processor with a slicing attachment on its thinnest setting or a mandolin – in this context not a musical instrument but a hand-operated slicing tool.

2 Put 1 tablespoon of the olive oil to warm in a large heavy frying pan. Mix the potatoes, leeks, lemon thyme, salt, pepper and the remaining oil together in a large bowl, turning them over gently with your hands to separate them and distribute the oil evenly throughout. Put about half the vegetables in the frying pan, spreading them evenly to cover the bottom of the pan. Try to make a completely impervious layer.

3 Now arrange the mozzarella to form the middle layer, sprinkle the Parmesan on top of that, then top it off with the remaining vegetables. Cover the pan with a lid, turn the heat down low and cook for about 40 minutes.

4 Now for the fun part – turning it all over! Loosen the potatoes gingerly from the base of the pan using a thin spatula. Shake the pan a little to make sure no sticky patches remain. Invert a large dinner plate over the pan, turn the whole lot upside down together and tip the contents of the pan onto the plate. In theory you should now be able to slide the potatoes back into the pan in one unbroken layer, but I rarely manage it. Put it back in as best you can and cook the other side for about 20 minutes over a gentle heat until all is meltingly tender and oozing with cheese.

SERVES 4 FOR DINNER, 6 OR MORE AS A SIDE DISH

Rocket bubble and squeak

A large panoply of dishes comprise combinations of mashed potato with various leafy green vegetables. Here is a particularly tasty variation with a contemporary twist. It has the added virtue of being able to hold quite well in a warm oven for up to half an hour – useful if the main course is one that requires last minute attention.

- 800 g floury potatoes, peeled
- 100 ml milk
- salt and pepper
- 1 large onion, peeled and chopped
- 15 g butter
- 1 tablespoon olive oil
- 4 cloves garlic, peeled and crushed
- 100 g rocket, chopped

1 Boil the potatoes in salted water until tender, then drain and mash them thoroughly. Beat in the milk (plus an extra lump of butter if you're feeling reckless) and season to taste with salt and pepper.

2 In a wide, shallow pan fry the chopped onion in the butter and olive oil, stirring occasionally, until tender and slightly browned. Add the garlic for the last couple of minutes. Add the chopped rocket to the pan and cook very briefly, then add the mashed potato and cook, stirring, until hot.

SERVES 4

VARIATION

Topped with slices of Chêvre Blanc goat's cheese log and finished under a hot grill, this makes a satisfactory main meal in itself, with an accompanying leafy salad.

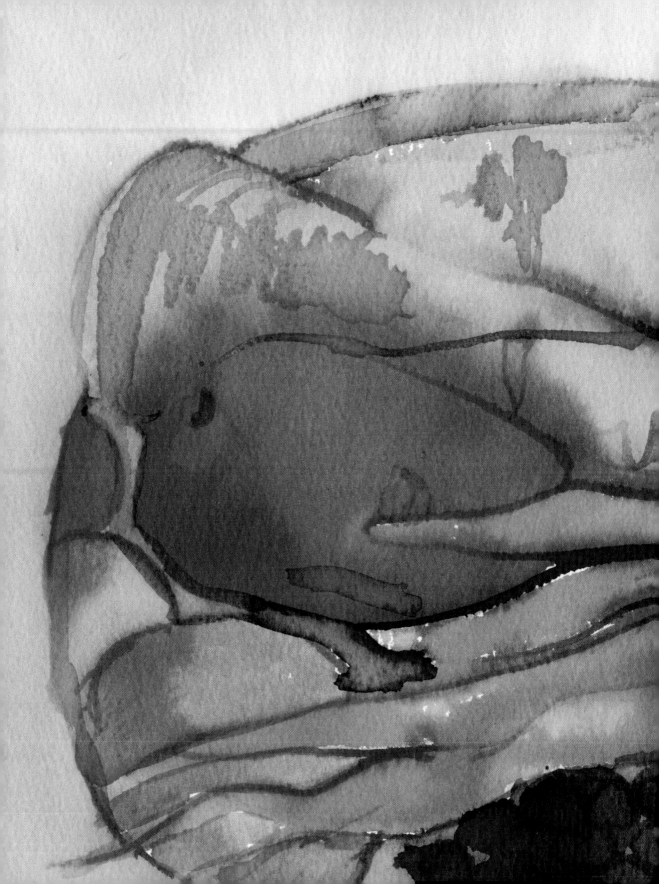

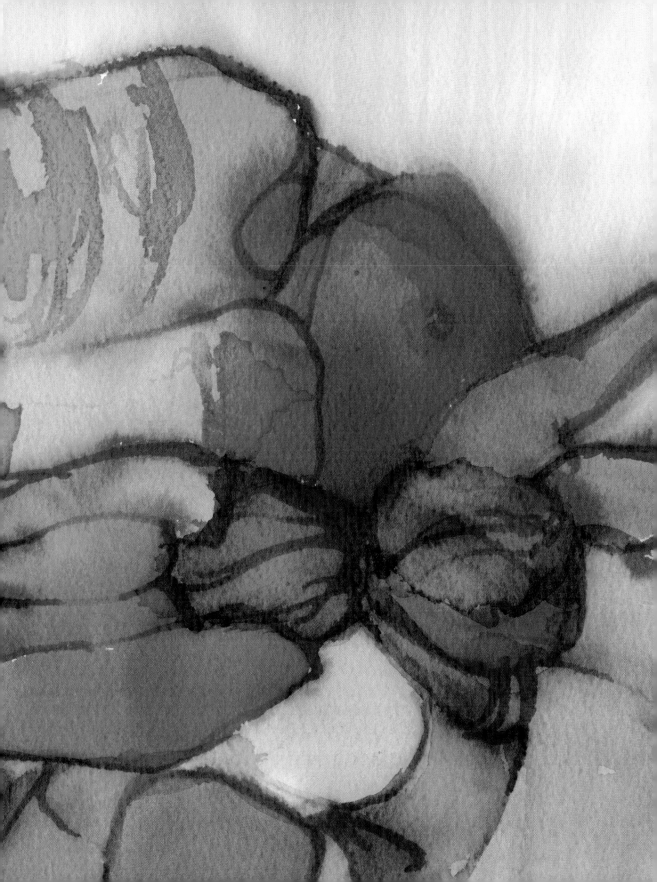

Root vegetable cakes

This is an oven-baked version of *rösti*. It makes quite a nice, simple winter supper served with poached eggs or dollops of very fresh cottage cheese and a crisp green salad.

- 220 g potatoes
- 110 g carrots
- 110 g parsnips
- 30 g butter, plus a little extra, melted, to brush over the cakes before baking
- 1 tablespoon olive oil

- 1 teaspoon cumin seeds
- 1 large onion, peeled and finely chopped
- 1 fresh red chilli, de-seeded and finely chopped (more or less, to taste)
- salt and pepper

Oven temperature: 200°C (400°F, gas 6) – adjust for fan ovens

1 Peel the potatoes, carrots and parsnips. Cut the potatoes and carrots into large even-sized chunks and boil in salted water for 5 minutes. Drain them, set aside until they are cool enough to handle, then grate the potatoes, carrots and raw parsnips. I use the medium blade on my food processor grating attachment. If you grate the vegetables too coarsely the cakes tend to fall apart.

2 Warm the butter and olive oil in a wide, shallow pan and fry the cumin seeds and chopped onion over a moderate heat for 5–10 minutes, until the onions are quite soft. Add the chilli and fry for a further 2–3 minutes. Combine the onion with the potatoes, carrots and parsnips and season with salt and pepper.

3 Place the mixture in heaped tablespoons on a well-buttered baking tray and press down with the back of a spoon. This method will give a slightly ragged outline that has its own charms but, if you want the cakes to be neater, oil the inside surface of a circular biscuit cutter and use it as a mould. Put the cutter on the baking tray, spoon some of the mixture inside it and squash down with the back of a spoon before carefully lifting off the cutter.

4 Brush the surface of each cake sparingly with melted butter, then bake in a pre-heated oven, middle shelf or above, for 25–30 minutes, until golden brown and slightly crisp around the edges.

MAKES 6–8 CAKES

Roasted roots with Parmesan

A good wintery side dish requiring no last minute attention, you could try this with *Pumpkin stew with coconut, chilli and coriander* (page 55).

- 400 g parsnips, peeled and quartered
- 500 g sweet potatoes, peeled and cut into chunks
- 200 g carrots, peeled and cut into chunks
- 150 g shallots, peeled and left whole
- 3 tablespoons olive oil
- 3 tablespoons balsamic vinegar
- salt
- 50 g grated fresh Parmesan cheese

Oven temperature: 220°C (425°F, gas 7) – adjust for fan ovens

1 When preparing the vegetables you should aim for chunks of a similar size. Bring a large pan of salted water to the boil and simmer the parsnips, sweet potatoes and carrots for 7 minutes, then drain them thoroughly.

2 Place the part-cooked vegetables in a large roasting tin with the uncooked shallots, olive oil and balsamic vinegar. Mix everything together gently but thoroughly so the vegetables are evenly coated with oil and vinegar. Spread the vegetables out in a single layer, sprinkle with a little salt and roast for about 45 minutes, turning occasionally, until all the vegetables are tender and flecked with brown.

3 Scatter the vegetables with the grated Parmesan and return the dish to the oven for a further 5 minutes, until the cheese has melted.

SERVES 4

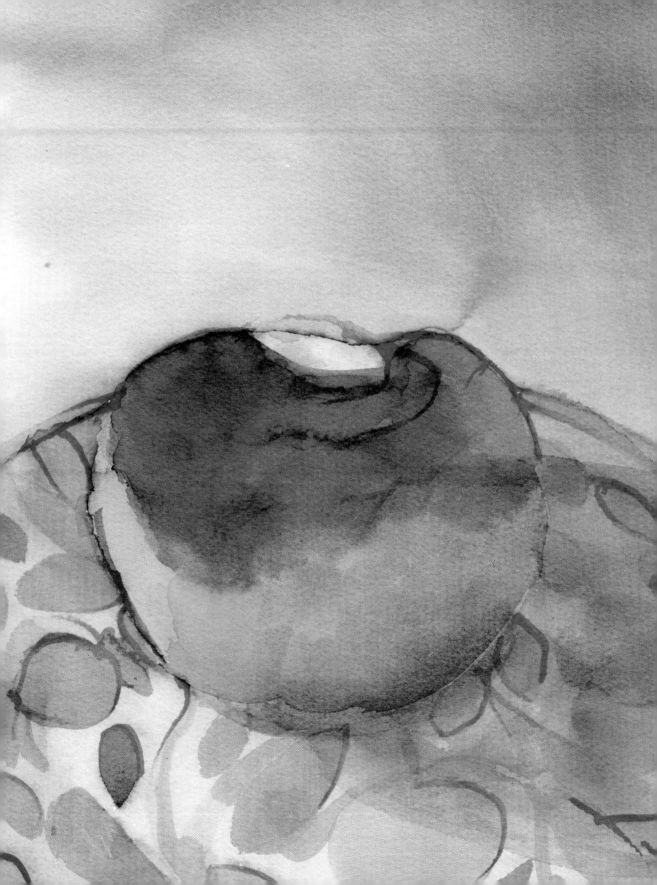

Swede and carrot mash with garlic and cumin

Spiced with cumin, this modern take on an old favourite is a savoury, wintry vegetable side dish, which has the virtue of being able to sit quite happily in a warm oven for up to half an hour without deterioration. This makes it a useful accompaniment to any number of main course dishes that require precise timing or last minute fiddling about of some sort. It's also one of those dishes that tastes even better re-heated the next day – the cumin flavour gets stronger.

- 300 g carrots, peeled
- 1 small swede, thickly peeled
- 1 large or 2 small onions, peeled and chopped
- 30 g butter
- 1 tablespoon olive oil

- 2 teaspoons cumin seeds
- 2 or 3 cloves garlic, peeled and crushed
- salt and pepper
- 2 or 3 tablespoons thick cream (optional)

1   Dice the carrots and swede and boil them separately until very tender. You can cook them in the same pan with a separator – the only reason to keep them apart is that they will probably take different times to cook. Both should be tender almost to the point of disintegration for this recipe, in order to get a smooth mash.

2   Meanwhile fry the chopped onions in the butter and olive oil until tender and starting to brown. Add the cumin seeds and garlic, fry a few minutes more, then set aside the pan and its contents for later.

3   When the swede and carrots are cooked, drain them thoroughly and put them back in the pan over the heat for a couple of moments to dry them off (shake the pan to dry them evenly and prevent burning). If you want the mash to be perfectly smooth put the swedes and carrots through a potato ricer or, alternatively, put them in a food processor and whiz for a few minutes, stopping the machine and scraping the mixture down from the sides as necessary. If the odd lump doesn't bother you, mash them in the pan using a potato masher.

4   Stir the mash into the pan containing the onions and season to taste with salt and pepper. Add the cream if you're using it. Re-heat gently in the pan, or turn into a shallow baking dish and warm in the oven, before serving.

SERVES 4

DESSERTS

Baked peaches with raspberries, marzipan and Amaretto

Here is a beautiful dessert for early autumn. Peaches should still be at their best and autumn-fruiting raspberries will carry on until the first frosts, but the weather is turning and cooler days make us want warmer food. This recipe takes all of five minutes to put together and may be assembled in advance, yet is sophisticated enough to make a good dinner party dessert. Serve it hot with cold, thick cream. Shop-bought marzipan is fine here if you're in a hurry but since home-made is nicer, and also very quick and easy to make, I've included a recipe overleaf.

- a little butter for the baking dish
- 4 perfect ripe peaches, washed, halved and stoned
- 100 g raspberries
- 4 teaspoons caster sugar
- 2 tablespoons Amaretto liqueur
- 200 g marzipan
- thick cream to serve

Oven temperature: 180°C (350°F, gas 4) – adjust for fan ovens

You will need a shallow baking dish large enough to hold the peach halves in a single layer.

1 Butter the baking dish and put in the peaches skin-side down. Mix together the raspberries, sugar and Amaretto, crushing the raspberries slightly. Share them out between the peaches, packing them into the cavities left by the stones.

2 Roll out the marzipan between sheets of greaseproof paper to about 5 mm thickness, peel off the top sheet of paper and stamp out peach-sized circles using a biscuit cutter (or an inverted glass). Put the marzipan lids on the peach halves and press down around the edges. Bake in a pre-heated oven for about 25 minutes, until the marzipan is slightly browned and the fruit fragrant. Don't forget the cream.

SERVES 4 VERY GENEROUSLY, 8 AFTER A LARGE MEAL

Amaretto marzipan

- 250 g ground almonds
- 250 g icing sugar, sifted
- 1 egg, lightly beaten
- 1 teaspoon natural almond essence
- Amaretto liqueur to mix

1 Mix together the almonds and sugar in a large bowl. Stir in the beaten egg and almond essence, then gradually add a few drops of Amaretto to bind the mixture. Don't over mix. It should come together quite easily – shape it into a ball with your hands. As with any recipe that contains raw eggs, this probably should not be given to the frail. Leftover marzipan may be wrapped in plastic and stored in the fridge.

MAKES JUST OVER 500 G

Espresso bread pudding with chocolate chunks

This is a useful cold-weather dinner party dessert but it requires a little forward planning. Day-old bread is a necessity as really fresh bread is unsliceable, and the pudding also needs to sit in the fridge for 24 hours before cooking, so we're talking two days' notice here. I make it with my favourite white bread, which happens to be the *Overnight bread* from my last book *VEG*, but a decent loaf from a craft baker would be fine.

As I don't like things too sweet this pudding might not be sweet enough for some tastes. It would almost certainly be too intense for most children. If this causes you concern increase the amount of sugar to 120 g. Serve the pudding with chilled thick cream.

- 40 g espresso coffee beans
- 280 ml carton double cream
- 160 ml milk
- 3 large eggs
- 100 g soft brown sugar, plus 1–2 tablespoons (but see note above)
- 250 g day-old white bread (about 6 slices off a medium loaf), sliced to sandwich thickness, crusts removed and cut into triangles
- 100 g dark chocolate, chopped into chunks

Oven temperature: 180°C (350°F, gas 4) – adjust for fan ovens

You will need a circular oven-proof dish, 23 cm in diameter and 6 cm deep, or something of a similar capacity.

1. Grind the coffee beans in an electric grinder, food processor or pestle and mortar very coarsely indeed. The briefest whiz is all that's required and they should still look very chunky when you've finished. Put the coffee, cream and milk in a small pan and heat gently to just below boiling point, stirring from time to time. Turn off the heat and set aside.

2. Whisk the eggs and sugar for 5–6 minutes until pale, thick and creamy, then strain the coffee liquid into them and mix thoroughly. Pour a little of the coffee custard into the bottom of the dish. Add a layer of bread triangles, keeping to a single thickness.

3. Sprinkle on some chocolate chunks. Pour on more coffee custard and continue layering in this fashion, finishing with chocolate chunks. If the bread is not fully submerged in coffee custard, press it down gently with the back of a spoon until it is. Cover the dish with cling-film, refrigerate and leave it all to soak for 24 hours before baking.

4. Remove the pudding from the fridge 2–3 hours before cooking, to bring it to room temperature. Sprinkle a tablespoon or two of brown sugar over the top and bake for 20–25 minutes in a pre-heated oven, middle shelf, until the pudding is crisp on top but still slightly runny in the centre.

SERVES 6–8

Baked buttered plums in Marsala

I made this one day when the delectable-looking imported organic plums I impulse-bought from the supermarket turned out to be rather insipid. They definitely needed jazzing up, and this worked a treat, transforming them into a more than acceptable hot dessert.

- 15 g butter
- 500 g large plums such as Santa Rosa, halved and stoned
- 40 g soft brown sugar
- 1 level teaspoon ground cinnamon
- 120 ml sweet Marsala
- chilled cream or Greek yogurt to serve

Oven temperature: 200°C (400°F, gas 6) – adjust for fan ovens

1 Use a little of the butter to grease the bottom and sides of an oven-proof dish. Arrange the plum halves, cut-side uppermost, in a single layer in the dish. Place a small piece of butter in the stone cavity of each plum half.

2 Mix together the sugar and ground cinnamon and sprinkle evenly over the fruit. Pour the Marsala carefully into the dish between the fruit, so as not to wash off the butter or sugar.

3 Cover the dish with a well-fitting lid or foil and bake on the middle shelf of a pre-heated oven for something between 20 minutes and 1¼ hours, until the plums are soft and their skins wrinkling. The time plums take to cook varies enormously depending on their size, variety and degree of ripeness.

4 Remove the lid, baste the fruit with its cooking liquid and return the dish uncovered to the oven for 5–10 minutes to finish cooking. The liquid should be reduced to a concentrated syrup. Serve hot, with chilled cream or Greek yogurt.

SERVES 4

VARIATION

Soak a handful of dried baby figs in the Marsala overnight and cook with the plums. The contrast between fresh and dried fruit is rather good.

Baked quinces filled with marzipan

Quinces are a wonderful and under-rated fruit. They seem rather archaic and mysterious, probably because the plant breeders have largely left them alone. Hard, white and inedible raw, when cooked they release a heady perfume and are transformed into delicious, delicate, pink fluff. They can be grated into cakes, being particularly good in almond cakes, and also have an affinity with apples, to which they are related.

Not all quinces are alike. If you have an old garden containing a mature tree cherish it, no matter how untidy it looks, as it's quite likely to produce fruit of a better, more characterful flavour than some of the modern varieties. Quinces make a fleeting appearance in the better greengrocers in autumn and winter. Rural WI markets (run by the Womens' Institute) are a possible source of fruit and I have occasionally seen them for sale in Waitrose supermarkets.

- 2 huge or 4 small quinces
- 30 g butter
- 180 g marzipan, cut into 5 mm cubes (page 132)
- 8 teaspoons honey
- chilled cream, crème fraîche or Greek yogurt to serve

Oven temperature: 200°C (400°F, gas 6) – adjust for fan ovens

1. Core the quinces and cut them in half around their middles. Butter a ceramic baking dish and put the quince halves in it, in a single layer, cut sides up. Trim a thin slice off their bases if necessary to make them sit without wobbling. Fill the cavities with marzipan dice, leaving about a third of the marzipan for later, and drizzle 1 or 2 teaspoons of honey over each quince half. Dot the fruit with small pieces of butter, cover loosely with foil and bake, covered, for 1–1¼ hours, depending on the size of the quinces, until the fruit is quite tender.

2. Scatter the remaining marzipan dice on top of the fruit and return them to the oven, uncovered, for a further 10–15 minutes until the marzipan is nicely browned. Keep a careful eye on it during this last stage to make sure the honey doesn't burn. Serve hot with cold, thick cream, crème fraîche or Greek yogurt.

SERVES 4

Poached quince with cardamom and rosewater

The quince tree is among the first to flower in my small orchard and its flowering is an anxious time since, if it coincides with a hard frost, the flowers are damaged, the crop destroyed and my culinary plans for the autumn come to nothing. The flowering is brief but exhilarating, the branches covered thickly with tiny, tightly-furled buds like miniature pale pink umbrellas, which open to delicate, single blush-white flowers of great purity and charm. I count them in eager anticipation (the tree is still quite small!), calculating how many I might reasonably expect to stay the course to fruitdom. With hope triumphing over experience, I always imagine this number to be much greater than it eventually turns out to be.

- 750–800 g quinces, washed and dried
- 800 ml water
- 80 g sugar
- 10 whole cardamom pods, slightly crushed but not broken up
- approximately 2 tablespoons rosewater
- a slosh of Cointreau (optional)

1 Quinces are very hard when raw and need to be tackled accordingly. Arm yourself with a large and very sharp knife and cut the quinces into quarters. Cut out the cores, then cut each quarter vertically into slices about 1 cm wide. Lay each slice in turn flat on the chopping board and peel by slicing the skin off vertically. Collect up the cores and all the peelings, then simmer them in the water for about 30–40 minutes to extract the flavour. Strain and save the water and discard the trimmings.

2 Put the quince water back in the pan, add the sugar and crushed cardamom pods and stir until the sugar has dissolved. Lower the raw quince slices into the liquid, cover the pan and simmer for 2–2½ hours, until the quinces are tender and a delicate pink shade.

3 Lift the quinces out of their cooking liquid with a slotted spoon and, at the same time, fish out and discard the cardamoms. Turn up the heat under the pan and reduce the liquid by about two thirds, until you are left with a concentrated pink syrup. Take the pan off the heat and add the rosewater to the syrup. You may need a little more or less than the amount specified as I think the rosewater is available in different strengths, so add less to start, taste and add more until it's to your liking. Add a slosh of Cointreau if you're feeling that way inclined. The quinces are delicious either way, so it really is optional. Finally, strain the syrup through a sieve onto the cooked quinces.

4 Serve warm or cold, perhaps with *Lemon ice cream* (page 159) or just with Greek yogurt or cream.

SERVES 4

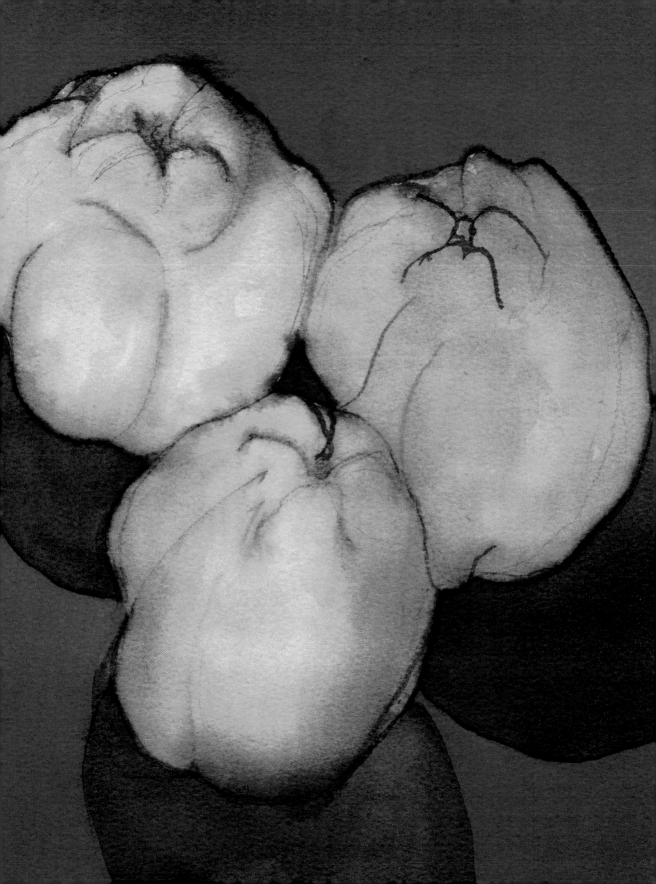

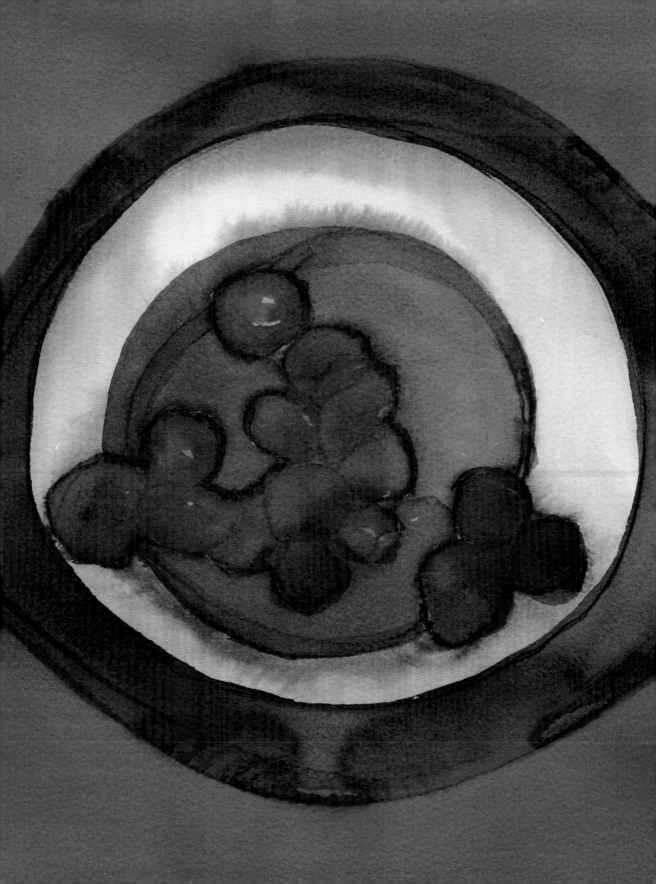

Damson clafouti with sloe gin syrup

Sadly the damson season is a short one. They are only around for a couple of weeks in August so snap them up if you see them or, better still, plant a tree and grow your own. This clafouti makes a lovely late summer dessert, served warm from the oven with a slosh of cold, heavy cream. A clafouti, in case you're wondering, is a cross between a pancake and a soufflé, baked in the oven and studded with fruit.

- 90 g soft brown sugar
- 90 ml sloe gin (use sweet Marsala wine if you can't get sloe gin)
- 300 g damsons, halved and stoned
- 50 g plain flour, sifted
- 50 g caster sugar

- 2 eggs, separated
- 40 ml milk
- 1 teaspoon natural almond essence
- pinch of cream of tartar (optional)
- ½ teaspoon baking powder
- a little butter for the baking dish

Oven temperature: 190°C (375°F, gas 5) – adjust for fan ovens

You will need an oven-proof dish about 25 cm diameter and at least 4 cm deep, buttered.

1 Put the brown sugar and sloe gin in a small saucepan and heat gently for a couple of minutes until the sugar has dissolved. Put the damsons in a shallow dish and pour over the hot syrup. Leave them to soak, turning them over occasionally so both sides are well-coated.

2 To make the clafouti batter, put the flour, caster sugar, egg yolks, milk and almond essence in a large bowl and beat with a whisk for a few minutes until the mixture goes quite pale and frothy. Whisk the egg whites in a clean dry bowl until they form snowy peaks. Add a pinch of cream of tartar if you have any – it helps to increase the volume.

3 At the last minute, whisk the baking powder into the egg and flour mixture, then gently fold in the egg whites. Pour about three quarters of this mixture into your buttered oven-proof dish and bake in a pre-heated oven, middle shelf, for 5 minutes to set the surface of the mixture and stop the plums from sinking. While the initial cooking takes place, drain the damson halves, saving the sloe gin syrup to pour on later.

4 Take the dish out of the oven and spread the remaining batter over the surface. Arrange the damson halves evenly, skin side up, and return the dish to the oven for 10–14 minutes until the batter is just set and the damsons cooked through. Pour over the sloe gin syrup and serve with cream.

SERVES 4

Individual Seville orange steamed puddings with a frangipane filling

These individual suet puddings make a fantastic cold-weather dessert for January or February. I love the flavour of bitter Seville marmalade oranges but their appearance in the shops is fleeting, lasting only about six weeks. Make the most of them while they're around – they are much too good to be confined to marmalade. In this recipe light and fluffy citrus puddings are filled with a fragrant, orange frangipane and served hot with chilled cream. If you've missed the boat for Sevilles, try the lemon version instead.

THE FRANGIPANE

- juice and grated zest of 2 Seville oranges
- 50 g butter
- 70 g caster sugar
- 1 egg yolk
- 100 g ground almonds
- 1 tablespoon plain flour
- 1 teaspoon natural almond essence
- 2 heaped teaspoons of Seville orange marmalade (preferably home-made)

THE PUDDING MIXTURE

- 200 g self-raising flour
- 200 g caster sugar
- a pinch of fine sea salt
- 1 teaspoon baking powder
- 100 g vegetarian suet
- grated zest and juice of 4 Seville oranges
- cream to serve

You will need six ramekins, individual pudding basins or teacups (180 ml capacity each), and a steamer large enough to hold the ramekins level in a single layer.

THE FRANGIPANE

1   Put the Seville orange juice in a small saucepan and cook, uncovered, until it is reduced in volume to about a tablespoon. Put the concentrated orange juice, butter, sugar, egg yolk, almonds, flour, grated orange zest and almond essence into a food processor and whiz until smooth, scraping the mixture down from the sides at intervals, as necessary.

2   Add the marmalade and whiz briefly, so it gets mixed in but some chunks of peel are retained. The mixture may be slightly runny. If so, put it in the fridge for a while. When it has stiffened up divide the mixture into 6, roll into balls and chill until needed.

3 Mix the flour, sugar, salt, baking powder, suet and orange zest together in a large bowl. Using the flat of the blade of a round-ended knife to mix everything, add the juice little by little until the mixture comes together in a soft dough. Depending on the oranges, you may have either too much or too little juice to bind the mixture. If the mixture is too dry just add a tiny amount of cold water but be careful not to add too much liquid – the dough should be quite stiff.

4 Put your hands in cold water for a few minutes to cool them before assembling the puddings. Essentially you are making suet pastry, and all pastry is best made at a cool temperature. Knead the dough very lightly using your hands, just enough to make it stick together. The less you handle it, the better the end result will be.

5 Divide the dough into six equal portions. Working with your hands well-floured, shape a portion of dough into a ball and flatten it out between your hands to make a circle of dough about 10 cm across. Place the flattened dough in the palm of one hand, then put a chilled ball of frangipane (from stage 2) in the centre of the circle. Gather up the edges and pinch them together to seal. Roll the filled pudding gently in your hands to get a good spherical shape. Place each pudding into a ramekin with the seal at the bottom. Cover each pudding tightly with a lid made from buttered baking foil. Tie on the lids with string to make a waterproof seal.

6 Place the ramekins in a steamer so they are suspended over boiling water, cover with a lid then steam for 1½ hours, topping up the boiling water if necessary. To serve, leave the puddings in the containers in which they were cooked. Your guests should make holes in the tops of their puddings and pour in the cream.

SERVES 6

VARIATION – LEMON PUDDINGS

Replace the 6 Seville oranges used in the recipe with 4 lemons. When making the pudding mixture replace the Seville orange zest and juice with the grated zest and juice of 2 lemons.

To make a lemon frangipane, omit the Seville oranges and the marmalade from the ingredients given, substitute the zest and juice of 2 lemons and add an extra 20 g caster sugar.

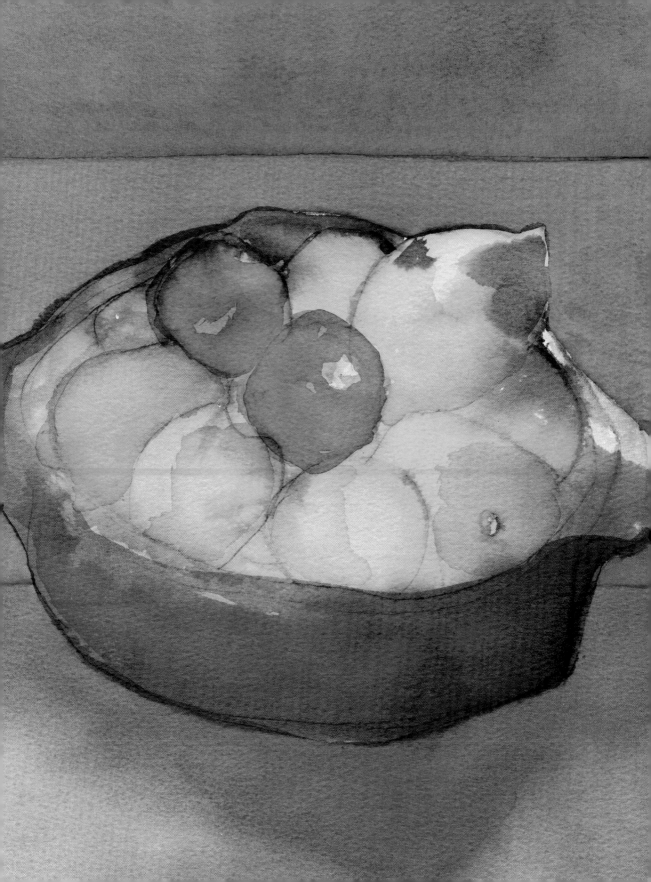

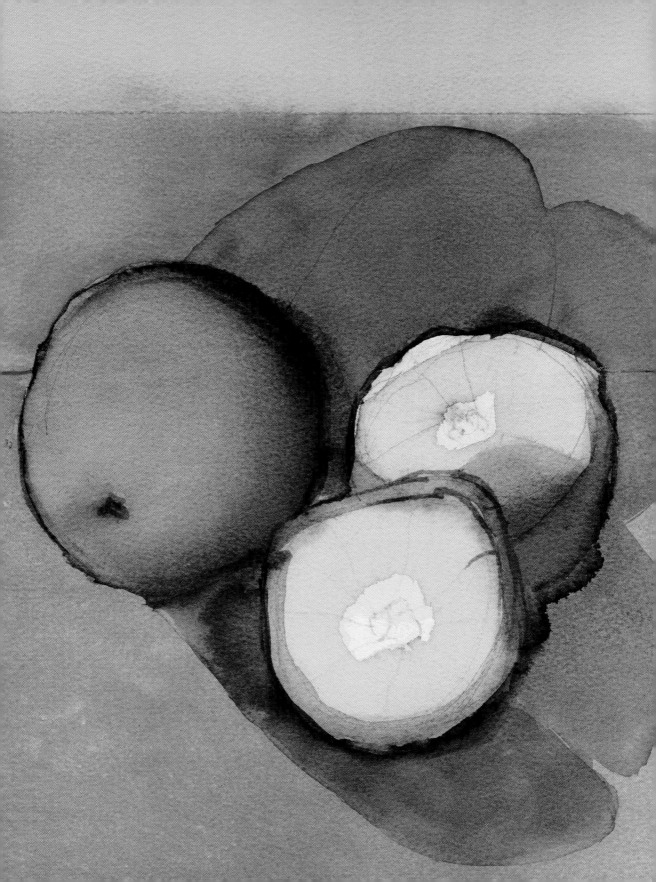

Raspberry and Amaretti cream pots

This is a heavenly summer or autumn dessert and just about as simple to make as it could possibly get. It needs to sit in the fridge for about an hour before serving to allow the biscuit crumbs to soften slightly and soak up the fragrant, red juices.

With raspberries more than any other fruit, to wash or not to wash is the dilemma – contact with water makes them turn to mush. Chemically produced crops may have pesticide residues, so buy organic, grow your own or put up with watery raspberries, but at least make an informed choice. . .

- 120 ml double cream
- 200 g raspberries
- 1 tablespoon caster sugar
- 60 g Amaretti biscuits

1 Whip the cream to the point where it just starts to hold its shape – it shouldn't be too stiff. Set aside three perfect raspberries for a garnish, then sprinkle the sugar on the remaining raspberries, squashing them very slightly with the back of a spoon.

2 Crush the Amaretti biscuits coarsely then stir them into the raspberries. Gently and partially fold in the whipped cream – leave the mixture a bit streaky. Spoon into three individual ramekins or glasses, chill for at least 1 hour before serving and garnish with the reserved raspberries.

SERVES 3

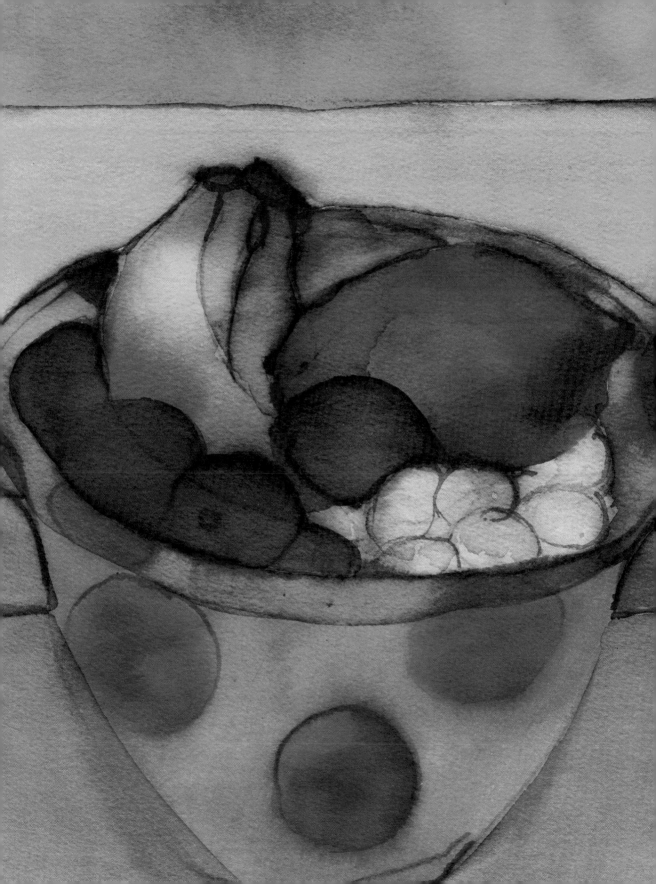

Ice creams, sorbets and yogurt ices

Home-made ices have an intensity that you rarely find in their shop-bought counterparts. Commerce dictates too long a shelf life and flavour diminishes over time, even in the best storage conditions. Fruit-based ices are particularly susceptible to this, I have found, and all the ices included here are best consumed within about 48 hours of making. They don't go off but the intensity of flavour diminishes quite quickly.

All the following recipes can be made in an ice cream machine if you own one, however, you don't need a machine to make good home-made ice creams or sorbets. It helps if you have an electric food mixer or a food processor, although again neither is essential – you can get by with just a fork. You will also need a wide shallow plastic or stainless steel dish or tray, preferably with a lid, that will fit in your freezer.

The single most important factor for success is probably the speed at which freezing takes place. This is influenced both by the temperature of your freezer and the size of the container holding the mixture. The faster that freezing happens, the smaller the ice crystals and the better the texture of the finished product, so if your freezer has a fast-freeze facility it's a very good idea to use it. It usually has to be turned on a few hours in advance to allow the temperature to fall.

Make your sorbet or ice cream mixture according to the individual recipe instructions and chill thoroughly before freezing. Pour the mixture into a wide, shallow dish, cover with foil or a lid and put it in the coldest part of the freezer. After 1 to 2 hours, the mixture will have started to freeze around the edges. The speed at which this happens depends on the efficiency of your freezer, the size of dish used and so on, so the timings given are approximate. Check after an hour, as you need to catch the mixture at the right moment when some ice has formed but before it is entirely solid.

Remove the dish from the freezer and beat the contents vigorously to break up the ice crystals. Use a food mixer or processor if you have one, otherwise an egg-beater or a fork. Return the dish to the freezer and repeat the beating twice more at 30 to 60 minute intervals.

To serve the ice immediately, return it to the freezer for about half an hour after its final beating to firm up. Most ices that have been in the freezer for several hours will need to be placed in a fridge to soften slightly for about half an hour before serving, although ices containing alcohol are usually soft enough to serve straight from the freezer.

Blackberry yogurt ice

I make this in late summer with wild hedgerow blackberries, which have a better flavour than their cultivated counterparts. Both this and the sorbet that follows are pretty intense, both in flavour and colour.

- 450 g blackberries
- 150 g caster sugar
- juice of half a lemon
- 450 g full fat Greek cow's yogurt

1 Wash and drain the blackberries. Purée them in a blender or food processor, add the remaining ingredients and push the mixture through a nylon sieve to remove the seeds. If you have an ice cream machine follow the manufacturer's instructions, otherwise follow the detailed freezing instructions on page 149.

SERVES 4

Blackberry sorbet

- 450 g blackberries, washed and drained
- 100 ml water
- 220 g caster sugar
- juice of a lemon

1 Cook the blackberries in the measured water in a covered pan over a gentle heat for 10–15 minutes until tender. Add the sugar and lemon juice and stir until the sugar has dissolved.

2 Mash the berries with a potato masher or fork, then push the fruit purée through a nylon sieve leaving the seeds behind. Taste and add a little more lemon juice or sugar if it seems necessary. If you have an ice cream machine follow the manufacturer's instructions, otherwise follow the detailed freezing instructions on page 149.

SERVES 4

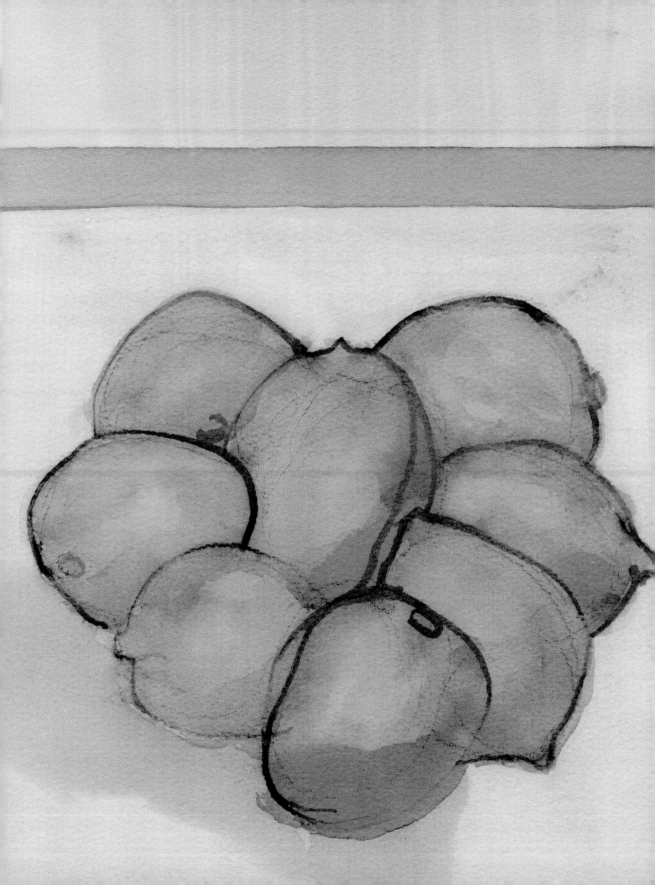

Chocolate, lime and Mascarpone ice cream

This ice was partly inspired by a fond nostalgia for the chocolate lime boiled sweets of my childhood. I liked them for their appearance as much as their flavour. Over-the-top synthetic green mini-lime shapes, with an intense dark chocolate centre – a perfect colour and flavour combination. The Mascarpone cheese crept in as a result of a liking for lime cheesecake and a desire to have the best of both worlds.

If you plan to make this in your freezer without an ice cream machine, re-member to turn the thermostat down to its coldest setting a couple of hours in advance. It makes quite a difference to the texture of the finished ice.

- 6 limes
- 250 g Mascarpone cheese
- 110 g icing sugar
- 100 ml milk
- a few drops of green food colouring (optional)
- 100 g dark chocolate (70% cocoa solids), well chilled and very finely chopped

1 Using a small and very sharp knife, peel all the skin and pith from 2 limes. Cut down the side of each segment and remove the lime flesh, leaving all the skin behind. Chop the denuded lime segments into very small pieces, spread them out in a freezer-proof container, cover and freeze them. They will be stirred into the ice cream later to provide crunchy little taste explosions!

2 Scrub the remaining limes, dry them and remove the zest with a zester or using the finest blade of a hand grater, then juice them and strain the juice.

3 Put the Mascarpone cheese, icing sugar and milk in a food processor and process briefly on medium speed, then pour the lime juice and zest through the spout into the machine while it is running. Add the food colouring if you're using it. I've included it largely for reasons of nostalgia (see above) and it's only necessary if you crave that synthetic green look!

4 If you have an ice cream machine follow the manufacturer's instructions, oth-erwise follow the detailed freezing instructions on page 149. When the ice is almost set stir in the frozen lime chunks and chopped chocolate.

SERVES 6

Damson and sloe gin sorbet

Sloe gin makes an excellent flavouring for all things plummy, sloes being a type of small wild plum. It is available commercially, although it's probably more often encountered in a home-made state. It also has the advantage of keeping the sorbet soft enough to serve straight from the freezer. Don't be tempted to add more sloe gin than stated in the recipe, otherwise the sorbet may not set.

- 300 g damsons
- 200 ml water
- 240 g caster sugar
- 1 tablespoon sloe gin

1 Wash the damsons and place in a saucepan with the measured water. Heat gently, stirring occasionally, and cook for about 10 minutes until the fruit is tender. Add the sugar and stir until dissolved.

2 Place the fruit in a food processor and whiz on quite a slow setting (use the pulse setting) to detach the flesh from the stones. Now press the fruit through a coarse nylon sieve using the back of a spoon, leaving just the stones behind.

3 If you have an ice cream machine follow the manufacturer's instructions, otherwise follow the detailed freezing instructions on page 149. Add the sloe gin towards the end of the freezing time, when the sorbet has started to solidify.

SERVES 4

Damson yogurt ice

Worth making for its colour alone, this simple, intense yogurt ice tastes as good as it looks.

- 300 g damsons
- 150 g caster sugar
- 450 g Greek yogurt
- 150 ml single cream

1 Wash the damsons and place in a saucepan. Heat gently, stirring occasionally, and cook for about 10 minutes until the fruit is tender. Add the sugar and stir until dissolved.

2 Place the fruit in a food processor and whiz briefly on a slow setting. The idea is to detach the damson flesh without actually breaking the stones or the food processor. Add the yogurt and cream and whiz briefly.

3 Now press this mixture through a coarse nylon sieve using the back of a spoon, leaving just the stones behind. Still freeze according to the instructions on page 149 or churn in an ice cream machine.

SERVES 4–6

Piña colada sorbet

A dessert with a decidedly retro feel, this would be fun to serve at a 70s party, but it's delicious enough to merit a trial run first. The coconut milk powder can be found in wholefood and oriental food shops and gives an excellent flavour.

- 130 g coconut milk powder
- 130 g caster sugar
- juice of 2 lemons

- 500 g fresh pineapple chunks (prepared weight – you'd need about a 600 g pineapple to yield this amount)
- 6 tablespoons white rum

1 Dissolve the coconut milk powder and sugar in a large measuring jug by adding a little boiling water. Give it all a good stir, then add cold water if necessary to make the liquid up to 300 ml.

2 Put the pineapple in a blender or food processor and whiz until smooth. Add the lemon juice and sweetened coconut liquid, then freeze.

3 If you have an ice cream machine follow the manufacturer's instructions, otherwise follow the detailed still freezing instructions on page 149. Either way, stir in the rum when the sorbet has begun to solidify. Don't be tempted to add extra rum or your sorbet may never set.

SERVES 6

Stem ginger ice cream

This is a traditional-style ice cream with a custard base and takes a bit longer to prepare than some of the yogurt ices and sorbets in this chapter. It tastes luxurious and would make a good dinner party dessert, particularly if served with small wedges of *Ginger and lemon fridge cake* (page 172). If you plan to still freeze this ice cream turn the freezer down to its coldest setting a couple of hours before you want to begin. There is some background information on ice cream making on page 149.

- 1 vanilla pod
- 340 ml semi-skimmed milk
- 90 g granulated sugar
- 4 egg yolks

- 3 tablespoons ginger syrup from a jar of preserved stem ginger
- 280 ml (250 g) double cream
- 6 walnut-sized pieces preserved stem ginger in syrup, finely diced

1 Split the vanilla pod lengthwise with a sharp knife and put it in a small, heavy saucepan. Pour on the milk, add half the sugar and bring it all almost to boiling point. Take the pan off the heat and leave it to infuse for at least 15 minutes.

2 Meanwhile, beat the egg yolks and remaining sugar, preferably with an electric whisk, at high speed for several minutes, until the mixture goes pale, thick and creamy. With an electric whisk this takes about 10 minutes, by hand, considerably longer.

3 Bring the sweetened, flavoured milk back to boiling point, then pour it onto the beaten egg yolks in a thin and steady stream, stirring as you do so. Now return the custard and vanilla pod to the pan and heat quite gently, stirring constantly with a wooden spoon, until the mixture thickens enough to coat the back of the spoon. Don't get distracted during this stage since, if the custard over-heats, it will turn into scrambled eggs and may be unsalvageable. Have a bowl of cold water ready and, as soon as the custard thickens, plunge the base of the pan into it so that cooking ceases immediately.

4 Leave the pan in the water, stirring occasionally, until the custard is cool, then transfer the custard to a shallow, plastic, lidded container and put it in the fridge to chill. When it is thoroughly cold, remove the vanilla pod and scrape the seeds into the custard using the point of a knife. Discard the empty pod and stir the ginger syrup and the cream into the custard. Either churn the mixture in an ice cream machine or still freeze following the detailed instructions on page 149. Stir in the diced stem ginger when the ice cream starts to solidify.

SERVES 6–8

Lemon ice cream

For anyone with a weakness for lemons this is an absolute stonker of an ice cream and, with just four ingredients, most definitely exemplifies the adage that less can be more. Its lively lemon taste rings out loud and clear. It's good enough to stand alone but, for a citroholics' dinner party dessert, it would be sensational with *Individual Seville orange steamed puddings with a frangipane filling* (page 142) in either its Seville orange or lemon incarnation.

The recipe calls for vanilla sugar, which is simple to make and a useful thing to have in the cupboard. Place a vanilla pod in a large screw-topped jar, half fill with caster sugar and give it a good shake. The sugar should be sufficiently vanilla-flavoured to use after two or three days. Leave the vanilla pod in the jar permanently, replenishing the sugar as you use it. I usually chuck out the pod and start again about once a year.

- 4 large organic, unwaxed lemons, juice and zest
- 500 ml thick cream (30% fat)
- 4 egg yolks
- 200 g vanilla sugar

1. Wash and dry the lemons, then use a lemon zester to get long thin strips of lemon rind with no white pith attached. If you don't have one, just grate it off using a fine grater. Heat the cream to just below boiling point and add the lemon zest. Turn off the heat and allow to infuse while you do the rest of the preparation.

2. Beat the egg yolks and sugar together for about 10 minutes, using an electric mixer, until pale and frothy. You will use them to make a custard and prolonged beating at this point helps prevent the custard from curdling.

3. Re-heat the cream and lemon zest to boiling point, then gradually add it to the egg yolks, beating thoroughly between additions. When it has all been added, rinse out the pan and return the custard to it. Heat very gently, stirring constantly, until the mixture thickens to the point where it will coat the back of the spoon. Be very careful not to over-heat or you'll end up with scrambled eggs. Have a bowl of cold water ready and, as soon as the custard thickens, plunge the base of the pan into it, so that cooking ceases immediately. Allow it to cool, then chill it thoroughly in the fridge before freezing.

4. Stir the strained lemon juice into the custard, then freeze. If you have an ice cream machine follow the manufacturer's instructions, otherwise follow the detailed freezing instructions on page 149.

SERVES 6–8

Banana yogurt ice

This ice requires forward planning since to get a really intense banana flavour you need to use over-ripe bananas. Their skins should be almost completely brown before you even contemplate making this so be prepared to keep the bananas in the fruit bowl for up to a week. Have faith! Although the ingredients don't sound out of the ordinary this is a truly delicious recipe – one where the whole is definitely more than the sum of the parts!

- 6 very ripe bananas, peeled and broken up
- juice of 1 lemon
- 200 g vanilla sugar (see page 159)
- 200 g Greek yogurt (preferably cow's and certainly not low fat)
- 120 ml single cream

1. Put the bananas, lemon juice and vanilla sugar in a food processor and whiz until smooth. Add the yogurt and cream then process briefly, just enough to combine everything. If you don't have a food processor just mash the bananas as smoothly as possible, adding the lemon juice to prevent discolouration, then combine with all the other ingredients.

2. Either way, still freeze following the instructions on page 149 or churn the mixture in an ice cream machine.

SERVES 6

Rum toffee sauce

This sauce is very good served hot over *Banana yogurt ice*, above.

- 405 g can sweetened condensed milk
- 200 ml water
- 4 tablespoons dark rum
- juice of $\frac{1}{3}$–$\frac{1}{2}$ lemon
- 3 rounded teaspoons black treacle or molasses

1. Boil the condensed milk and water together in a heavy saucepan for 20 minutes over a moderate heat, stirring constantly. Don't worry if it goes slightly lumpy with bits of caramelized milk. The lumps soften and dissolve as the sauce cools.

2. Take the pan off the heat, allow to cool slightly and stir in the remaining ingredients. Taste, adding extra lemon juice if necessary. Pour the hot sauce over some cold ice cream and eat immediately. Alternatively, let the sauce cool completely, then pour into a jar and chill.

3. The sauce will solidify when cold. To make it runny again either heat it gently in a pan or stir in a little hot water from the kettle.

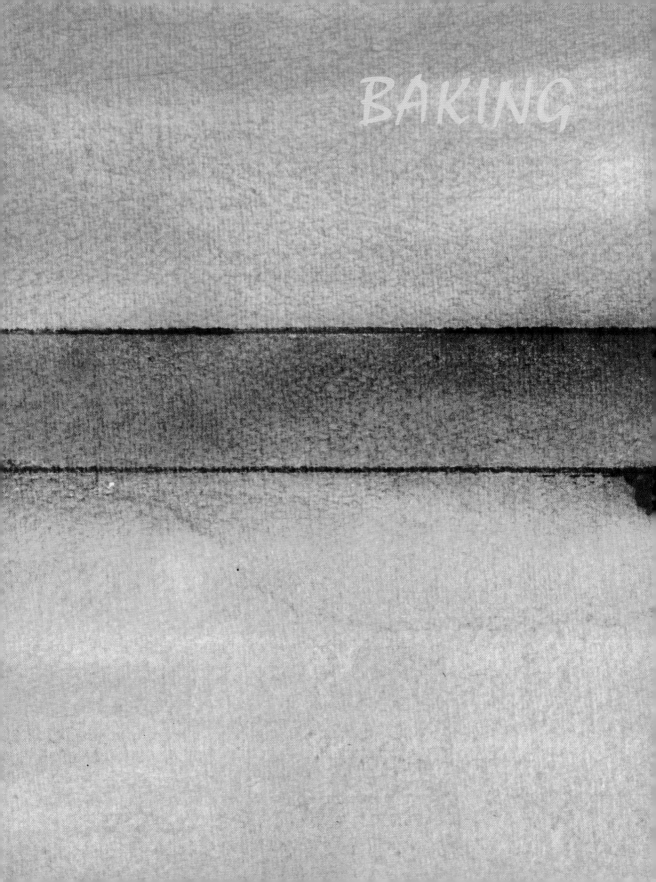

BAKING

Seville orange, Cointreau and walnut cake

This cake is beautifully moist, as a fruity syrup of Cointreau and concentrated bitter orange juice is poured over the hot cake just as it emerges from the oven. The syrup is made by stirring sugar and Cointreau into cold juice that has previously been simmered to concentrate the flavour. It's important to let the juice cool before adding the sugar as the sugar should not be completely dissolved. When the syrup is poured over the cake a crystalline layer forms on top giving it a slight crunch when it cools and sets.

- 8 Seville oranges, washed and dried
- 200 g walnut pieces
- 170 g butter at room temperature, plus a little extra for the cake tin
- 170 g caster sugar
- 110 g wholewheat flour
- 1½ level teaspoons baking powder
- ½ teaspoon ground cinnamon
- 4 eggs, lightly beaten with a fork
- 60 ml Cointreau
- 110 g soft brown sugar

Oven temperature: 170°C (340°F, gas 3½) – adjust for fan ovens

You will need a shallow cake tin 17 cm × 26 cm, or equivalent, buttered and lined with baking parchment. Don't use one with a removable base – it might leak.

1 Finely grate the zest from four of the oranges and put it in the food processor bowl for later, then juice all eight oranges. Strain the juice into a shallow, non-reactive saucepan and boil over a moderate heat for a few minutes until it is reduced to about 120 ml. Set it aside to cool. Coarsely chop 90 g of the walnuts and set aside for later.

2 Put the remaining 110 g walnuts in the food processor with the orange zest and whiz until they are finely ground, then add the butter, caster sugar, flour, baking powder and ground cinnamon to the food processor bowl. Process at slow to medium speed in short bursts until everything is well mixed, gradually adding the beaten egg through the food processor spout. Don't leave the machine running as the cake should not be over mixed.

3 Stir in the chopped walnuts by hand. Spread the mixture evenly in the prepared cake tin and bake in a pre-heated oven for 30–40 minutes until firm and golden brown. When cooked the cake should spring back when pressed lightly but if you are in any doubt insert a metal skewer into the centre. If it comes out clean the cake is done, if not give it a few minutes more.

4 While the cake is baking make the syrup by adding the Cointreau and soft brown sugar to the concentrated bitter orange juice. Stir to break up any lumps but don't try to dissolve the sugar. As soon as the cake comes out of the oven stab it all over with a narrow-bladed knife, then spoon the syrup evenly over the cake. Leave it to cool in the tin.

SERVES 8–10

Chocolate marzipan Amaretto cake

A dense but light, almondy chocolate sponge, studded with chunks of pale marzipan, laced with Amaretto liqueur and covered with a thick layer of fudgy chocolate frosting, this makes a good celebration cake. Apropos the marzipan chunks, there is a slight dilemma. If you cut them too small they virtually disappear into the cake mixture with a considerable lessening of impact, but if too large they tend to sink to the bottom of the cake. The biggest they can be without sinking is about 1 cm cubed.

THE CAKE

- 100 g dark chocolate (70% cocoa solids)
- 3 large eggs, separated
- 110 g butter
- 110 g sugar
- 2 teaspoons almond essence
- 90 g self-raising flour
- 90 g ground almonds
- 200 g marzipan, chilled and cut into 1 cm cubes – you could use *Amaretto marzipan* (page 132)
- 4 tablespoons Amaretto di Saronno liqueur

THE CHOCOLATE FROSTING

- 100 g dark chocolate (70% cocoa solids)
- 30 g butter
- 5 teaspoons sugar
- 2 tablespoons water

Oven temperature: 180 °C, 350 °F, Gas 4. Adjust for fan ovens, but if possible turn the fan off as it tends to dry the cake too much.

THE CAKE

1 The cake needs a 20 cm circular cake tin, preferably with a removable base. Prepare the cake tin by oiling the sides and base using butter or a very light oil such as peanut oil. Line the base with a circle of baking parchment – the butter will stick it down.

2 Melt the chocolate in a double boiler or heat-proof bowl suspended over barely-simmering water. As soon as it is fully melted, remove the chocolate from the heat and set it aside to cool.

3 Whisk the egg whites in a clean, dry bowl with a clean, dry whisk until they are stiff and snowy. Cream the butter and sugar together in a large mixing bowl until light and fluffy, then beat in the melted chocolate, followed by the egg yolks and almond essence, then the flour and ground almonds.

4 The mixture will be quite stiff at this point so, using a large metal spoon, stir in a dollop of egg white to slacken it. Now gently fold in the remaining egg whites, trying to lose as little air as possible from the mixture. Finally, stir in the marzipan cubes and spread the mixture into the prepared cake tin.

5 Bake in the middle of the oven for 40–60 minutes, until a skewer inserted into the centre of the cake comes out clean. Remove the cake from the tin and put it to cool on a wire rack. While it is still warm, sprinkle on the Amaretto. When the cake is completely cool, transfer it to its intended serving plate.

THE CHOCOLATE FROSTING

6 Put all the ingredients in a double boiler or heat-proof bowl suspended over barely-simmering water. Stir intermittently until everything has melted and amalgamated into a smooth, glossy sauce, then quickly pour it over the cake, tilting the cake to get it evenly coated. There is no need to use a knife – this frosting is self-spreading and will set to a lovely fudgy consistency in a few hours, a process which can be hastened in the fridge.

SERVES 6–8

Fig, orange and cardamom slice

This is an up-market variation on the old wholefood 'date slice' theme, with a generous, juicy layer of aromatic fig paste sticking everything together.

THE FIG LAYER
- 340 g dried figs, stalks removed
- 10 whole cardamom pods
- 170 ml fresh orange juice
- 50 g soft brown sugar

THE BASE
- 130 g butter
- 60 g soft brown sugar
- 170 g wholewheat flour
- 90 g rolled oats
- a pinch of salt

Oven temperature: 180°C (350°F, gas 4) – adjust for fan ovens

THE FIG LAYER

1 Put the figs, cardamoms and orange juice in a small saucepan and heat, stirring. Press down on the cardamom pods, crushing them slightly to help release their flavour. Cover the pan and simmer gently for about 15 minutes until the figs are plump and tender, then fish out the cardamom pods with a spoon and discard them. Put the contents of the pan in a food processor, add the sugar and whiz to a smooth paste.

THE BASE

2 Melt the butter and sugar in a large pan over a gentle heat. Take the pan off the heat, then stir in the flour, oats and salt. Mix thoroughly, using your hands if necessary. The mixture should look like coarse bread crumbs.

3 Press about two thirds of the crumbs into a circular cake tin of 20 cm diameter (or equivalent). I use one with a removable base. Spread the fig and orange purée evenly over the base. Sprinkle the remaining crumbs on top, pressing them into the purée, and bake for about 30 minutes, until lightly browned. Cool in the tin before slicing.

SERVES 8

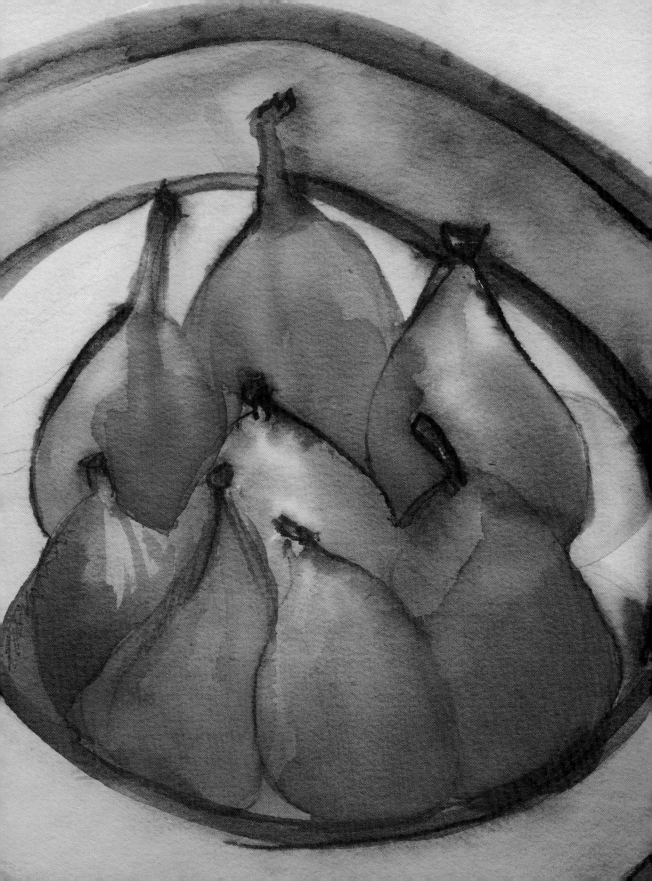

Coffee and walnut biscuits with white chocolate chunks

This recipe has caused me more problems than any other in this book. No matter what I did I couldn't get the coffee flavour strong enough. In the un-cooked mixture the coffee taste came through loud and clear, but after baking it virtually disappeared. I kept trying, increasing the amount of coffee each time, until eventually I arrived at a quantity that is enough to withstand the baking process. The uncooked mixture tastes very strong, but something weird happens during the baking process. The raw caffeine strength is tamed and the end result is a very 'more-ish' cookie with a good balance of flavours.

- 60 g coarsely chopped roasted walnuts
- 3 level tablespoons instant coffee granules
- 120 g butter at room temperature
- 150 g caster sugar
- 220 g self-raising flour (or use plain plus 3 level teaspoons baking powder)
- 1 egg
- 2–3 tablespoons milk (if mixture very stiff)
- 100 g white chocolate, coarsely chopped into chunks (I use Green and Blacks organic white chocolate, which is excellent)

Oven temperature: 180°C (350°F, gas 4) – adjust for fan ovens

1 To roast the walnuts spread them out in a single layer on a baking tray and cook for about 9 minutes in a pre-heated oven, until they start to smell toasty. Use a timer, as they burn very easily and, when done, set them aside to cool.

2 Dissolve the coffee granules in about 4 tablespoons of hot water from the kettle. Put the butter, sugar, flour, egg and coffee liquid into a food processor bowl and process at medium speed on a pulse setting until well mixed. Stop the machine and scrape the mixture from the sides of the bowl with a spatula if necessary. You may need to add a couple of tablespoons of milk if the mixture is very stiff.

3 Stir the white chocolate chunks and chopped walnuts into the mixture by hand, then drop teaspoons of the mixture onto a lightly buttered baking sheet and flatten slightly with the back of a fork. Keep the spacing quite wide as they will spread in the oven.

4 Bake in the middle of the oven for 15–20 minutes until golden brown, then cool on a wire rack. The biscuits are quite soft when they emerge from the oven but will crisp as they cool. If, when they're completely cold, the biscuits are still soft in the centre it's perfectly OK to re-heat the oven and put them back for a few more minutes to crisp up, although some people might prefer them slightly chewy. I think crisp comes top, just by a whisker.

MAKES ABOUT 24 BISCUITS

Ginger and lemon fridge cake

This dense, chewy ginger biscuit cake is very fast and simple to make. It is quite rich and intense in flavour so serve small wedges. It's very good with a tiny cup of strong espresso coffee.

If you can find the type of crystallized lemon peel that comes in large chunks it's better than the pre-chopped type used for cake making, but the latter will do at a pinch.

- 60 g crystallized lemon peel
- 60 g crystallized ginger
- 200 g Ashbourne ginger biscuits, or other crunchy ginger biscuits
- 1 large ripe lemon, scrubbed and dried
- 80 g butter
- sifted icing sugar to decorate

1 Coarsely chop the crystallized lemon peel, then put it and the crystallized ginger into a food processor and whiz until the chunks are quite small.

2 Add the ginger biscuits to the bowl and pulse whiz until they are quite well broken up but not yet reduced to fine crumbs. Grate the rind off the lemon, using a fine grater and add to the biscuit mixture.

3 Squeeze the lemon and simmer the juice in an open saucepan until it has reduced in volume to about a tablespoon. Add the butter to the pan and allow it to melt, then pour the lemon butter mixture into the crumb mixture. Mix well and press the mixture firmly into a 20 cm shallow cake tin. Chill in the fridge until set firm.

4 Put a little icing sugar in a sieve and sift evenly over the fridge cake before serving. Two tips – practice sifting over paper first, and perform the sifting process over a dry kitchen sink. Surplus icing sugar may then be rinsed down the plug hole, rather than covering the kitchen surfaces in sticky snow!

MAKES 8–12 PORTIONS

Chocolate and macadamia fridge cake

This dense, fudgy chocolate cake could hardly be easier. Just remember to soak the raisins in a little dark rum for at least 12 hours before you put it together. 60 g raisins will absorb about 2 tablespoons rum, but these rum-soaked raisins are so useful you may want to make extra to keep as a stand-by.

Roasting really brings out the flavour of nuts, and is worth the minimal effort it takes. To roast macadamia nuts pre-heat the oven to 180°C (350°F, gas 4) – adjust for fan ovens. Spread out the nuts in a single layer on a baking tray and cook for 9–12 minutes. Use a timer, as they burn very easily.

THE CAKE

- 120 g butter
- 4 heaped tablespoons cocoa
- 1 rounded tablespoon golden syrup
- 200 g digestive biscuits, roughly crushed
- 80 g roasted macadamia nuts
- 60 g rum-soaked raisins (see above)

THE CHOCOLATE ICING

- 100 g dark chocolate (around 70% cocoa solids)
- 5 level teaspoons vanilla sugar or caster sugar
- 30 g butter
- 2 tablespoons water

1 Melt the butter, cocoa and golden syrup over a gentle heat. Stir in the digestives, nuts and raisins. Turn the mixture into a lightly-oiled 20 cm round cake tin, preferably with a removable base, spread it out and press it down firmly.

2 To make the icing, put all the ingredients in a heat-proof bowl, suspended over a pan of barely-simmering water. Stir with a fork until melted and smooth, then pour over the cake. Tilt the cake tin from side to side so the covering spreads evenly over the surface. Refrigerate until set, then cut up.

MAKES 12 SMALL OR 8 LARGE PORTIONS

Lovage and onion bread

This is an intensely savoury loaf, a great accompaniment to cheese or soup, but quite delicious just with butter.

- 2 tablespoons olive oil
- 1 medium or 2 small onions, peeled and chopped
- 1 tablespoon sugar, plus a pinch
- salt and pepper
- 1 teaspoon fast-action dried yeast

- 300 g white bread flour
- ½ teaspoon salt
- 15 g fresh lovage leaves, washed, drained and finely chopped
- about 180 ml lukewarm water

Oven temperature: 190°C (375°F, gas 5) – adjust for fan ovens

1 Heat 1 tablespoon of the olive oil and fry the chopped onions, not too fiercely, until they are tender. Add a pinch of sugar to caramelize them towards the end of the cooking time. When the onions are soft and nicely browned season them to taste with salt and pepper and set them aside to cool.

2 Put the yeast, flour, salt, 1 tablespoon sugar and chopped lovage in a large mixing bowl. Add the remaining tablespoon of olive oil and most of the water and mix well, first with a wooden spoon, then change over to using your hands. Add more water if the mixture seems unmanageably dry. Tip the dough out onto a clean, lightly floured surface and knead for about 10–15 minutes, until the dough feels stretchy and satiny smooth.

3 Roll out the dough into a large rectangle, about 30 cm × 20 cm, and distribute the fried onions evenly over its surface, leaving a 15 mm margin around the edges. Brush this margin with water, then roll up the dough starting from one of the short sides and pinch the seams firmly closed.

4 Place the loaf seam side down in an oiled loaf tin or on a baking tray, cover with a damp tea towel and leave it in a warm, draught-free place such as an airing cupboard to rise until it has doubled in volume (1–2 hours depending on the conditions).

5 Bake in a pre-heated oven for about 18 minutes, then remove the loaf from the tin and return it to the hot oven directly on a shelf for a further 2–7 minutes, until the crust is golden brown and the bottom of the loaf makes a hollow sound when tapped with your knuckle. Cool on a wire rack.

MAKES 1 LOAF

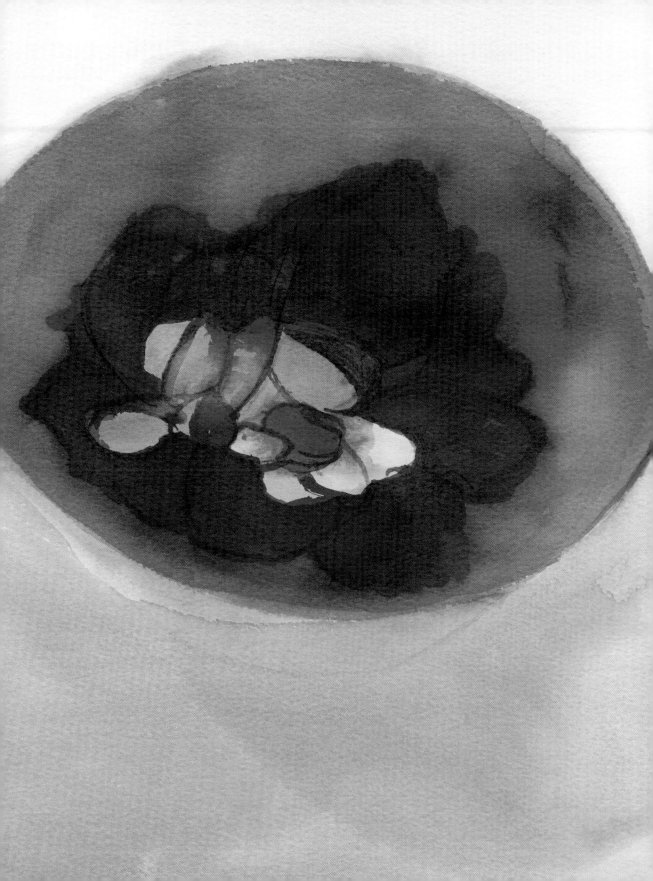

Basil and pistachio bread

This is a lovely, delicate bread and makes a nice accompaniment to salads or soups. If you need more than one loaf it's easy to make double quantity.

THE DOUGH

- 300 g white bread flour
- ½ teaspoon salt
- 1 teaspoon sugar
- ¾ teaspoon fast-action dried yeast
- 1 tablespoon olive oil
- 150–200 ml lukewarm water

THE FILLING AND GLAZE

- 15 g fresh basil leaves
- about 2 teaspoons olive oil
- a pinch of salt
- 50 g shelled, unsalted pistachio nuts
- a pinch of Maldon sea salt, or other flaky salt for the glaze

Oven temperature: 190°C (375°F, gas 5) – adjust for fan ovens

1 For the filling pound the washed basil leaves, 1 teaspoon olive oil and a pinch of salt in a pestle and mortar (or whiz in a food processor) to make a smooth, aromatic, green sludge. Set aside while you make the dough.

2 Put the flour, salt, sugar, yeast and 1 tablespoon olive oil in a large bowl and mix well. Gradually add lukewarm water until the mixture comes together to form a soft dough. The precise amount of water necessary will vary according to the flour used. Flour your hands and the work surface to prevent sticking, tip the mixture onto the work surface and knead until the dough is smooth, silky and elastic, which should take about 10 minutes. Add an extra sprinkle of flour occasionally if necessary. Flatten the dough into a large rectangle about 30 cm × 20 cm, either with your hands or a rolling pin.

3 Spread the basil paste over the dough, leaving a 15 mm bare margin along one short side and both long sides, then scatter with the pistachio nuts. Gently press the nuts into the dough using your fingers, just enough to make them stick. Moisten the dough margins with a little water, then roll up the dough Swiss-roll fashion, starting from the short side that has basil paste right up to the edge. Pinch the seam and ends very firmly closed using your fingers. Place the loaf seam side down on an oiled baking tray. Cover with a clean, damp tea towel and put it to rise in a warm, draught-free place such as an airing cupboard. Leave for about 1½–2 hours, until the dough has approximately doubled in size.

4 To glaze the loaf, lightly brush the surface of the risen dough with a little extra olive oil and scatter it with salt flakes. Bake in a pre-heated oven for 20–25 minutes until the crust is pale golden brown and the bottom of the loaf makes a hollow sound when tapped with your knuckle. Remove the loaf from the tin and return it to the hot oven directly on a shelf for a further 2–3 minutes to crisp the base.

MAKES 1 LOAF

BREAKFASTS AND SNACKS

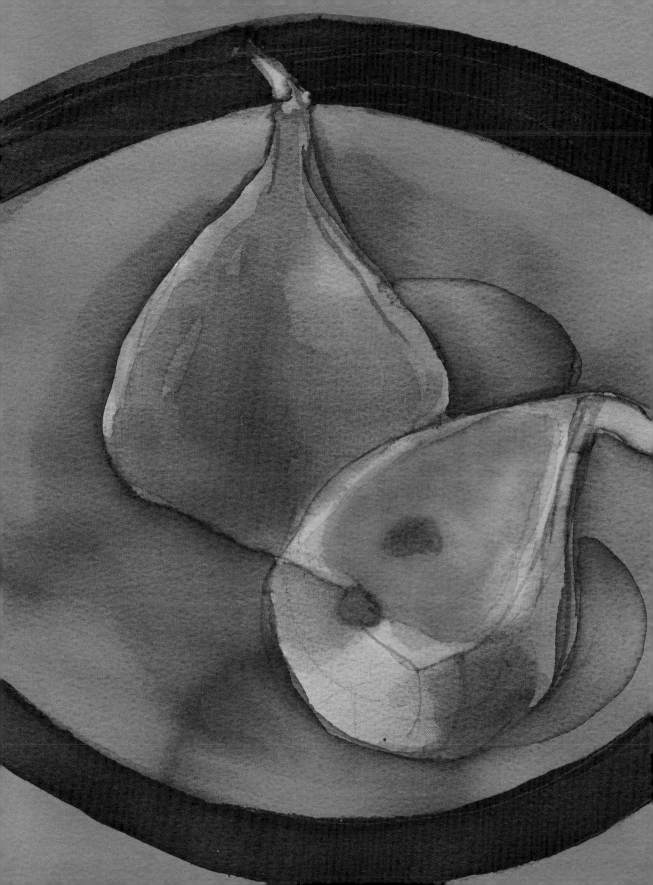

Two fig clafouti

Although it sounds like a character from an old John Wayne movie, this recipe is actually a delicious and soothing hot breakfast or brunch dish for a cool autumn morning. At a pinch it could double as a dessert, although I find the mixture of warm fruit and eggs particularly suited to the morning. The combination of fresh and dried figs tastes wonderful and also makes the expensive fresh figs go much further. If you can't find dried baby figs, use normal sized figs and cut them into quarters after soaking. Stir a spoonful of runny honey into a jug of thick Greek yogurt to serve alongside the clafouti.

- 120 g dried baby figs (but see note above)
- 3 luscious ripe fresh figs
- a scrap of butter for the baking dish
- 50 g self-raising flour, sifted
- 50 g caster sugar
- 2 eggs, separated
- 40 ml milk
- 1 teaspoon natural vanilla extract
- pinch of cream of tartar (optional)
- a sprinkling of icing sugar to garnish
- Greek yogurt and honey to serve

Oven temperature: 190°C (375°F, gas 5) – adjust for fan ovens
For this recipe you need a ceramic flan dish 30 cm in diameter or similar.

1. Put the dried figs to soak in boiling water while you prepare the other ingredients. Use just enough water to cover them. Prepare the fresh figs by snipping off the stalk ends. Cut them into quarters vertically, then cut each quarter in half to give triangular-ish chunks. Butter the flan dish.

2. Put the flour, caster sugar, egg yolks, milk and vanilla extract in a large bowl and beat with a whisk for a few minutes until the mixture goes quite pale and frothy. It will start out yellow and go noticeably paler.

3. Whisk the egg whites in a clean dry bowl until they form snowy peaks. Add a pinch of cream of tartar if you have any – it helps to increase the volume.

4. At the last minute, whisk the baking powder into the egg and flour mixture, then gently fold in the egg whites. Pour about three quarters of this mixture into the buttered oven-proof dish and cook for 3 minutes to set the surface of the mixture and stop the fruit from sinking.

5. Drain the dried figs, take the dish out of the oven and arrange both types of figs over the surface in a random but pleasing pattern. Pour the remaining batter mixture around them (the idea is for them not to be completely submerged) and return the dish to the oven for 12–15 minutes until the batter is just set. Sprinkle with icing sugar through a sieve before serving.

SERVES 2–3

Spiced plum, fig and orange compôte

This hot fruit compôte makes a lovely autumn breakfast on a slightly chilly morning. Plums are among the most beautiful of fruit, undeservedly neglected it often seems. The lovely old English and French varieties don't really fit the needs of the modern supermarket supply chain, being thin-skinned and somewhat averse to travel. In small country market towns each autumn, however, you can find glowing punnets of the jewel-like fruit, in a myriad shades of wine-red, amber, green and gold, all covered in a most delicate and perfect dusky bloom, which disappears the moment you touch them. With their luscious flavours, sensuous good looks and evocative varietal names (*Warwickshire Drooper*, *Coe's Golden Drop*, *Laxton's Blue Tit*, *Belle de Louvain*...), they deserve much greater respect than is usually afforded them and should be cause for national celebration!

Don't confine yourself to the ubiquitous *Victorias*, delicious though they are. Try them all, even the sour, cooking varieties if you get the chance – the flavours can be astonishingly good. Farmers markets, Pick Your Own fruit farms, roadside stalls and even car boot sales have all proved good sources of the more unusual varieties in my part of the world.

Some plums are definitely more attached to their stones than others. If yours fall into this category just leave them whole, but remember to warn people.

- 100 ml fresh orange juice
- a handful of dried baby figs
- 4 cloves
- 3 cm stick of cinnamon
- 450–500 g plums, cut in half and stoned (but see above)
- 100 g soft light brown sugar

1 Put the orange juice, dried figs, cloves and cinnamon to warm in a wide frying pan with a lid, while you prepare the plums.

2 Add the plum halves to the pan in a single layer, bring to the boil, turn down the heat, cover and simmer very gently for about 10 minutes until the plums are cooked.

3 Push the plums to one side in the pan and add the sugar to the liquid, stirring until it has dissolved. Serve the compôte hot or warm with Greek yogurt.

SERVES 2–3

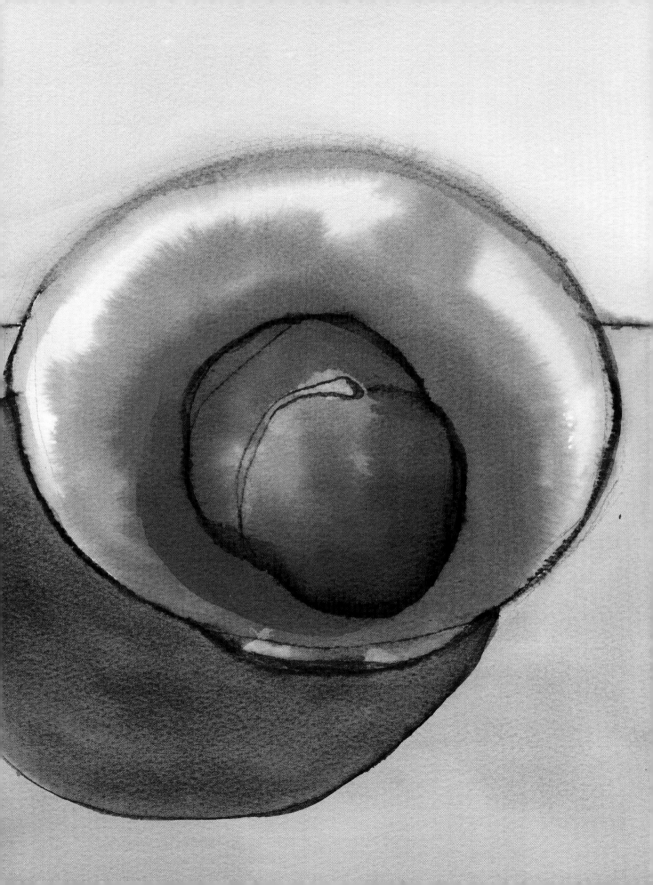

Strawberry yogurt shake

I make this strawberry yogurt milkshake through the winter from frozen strawberries. It makes a delicious breakfast drink and is the best way I know of using frozen strawberries. A taste of summertime first thing in the morning is somehow particularly welcome. Incidentally, if you want to freeze strawberries they keep their flavour much better if frozen whole rather than puréed.

If you make up a batch of strawberry purée as suggested here, there will be enough for several milkshakes that can then be made using a cocktail shaker or whisk without repeated recourse to the food processor. Rather than give quantities I am suggesting proportions, so you can more easily adapt the recipe to make the amount required. After you've made this a couple of times, you probably won't need to bother measuring the ingredients, as precision is unimportant here. The suggested proportions give quite a thick shake. If you'd prefer it thinner just add extra milk or cold water.

THE STRAWBERRY PURÉE

- 750 g strawberries, fresh or frozen and defrosted
- 150 g caster sugar
- the juice of a small lemon

TO MAKE UP THE MILKSHAKES

- 4 parts strawberry purée
- 5 parts milk
- 1 part Greek yogurt
- ½ teaspoon per serving of ground cardamom seeds to flavour (optional)
- ice cubes

1 Make the purée by whizzing all the ingredients together in a food processor or blender, then refrigerate it until needed.

2 Shake the milkshake ingredients vigorously with ice in a cocktail shaker, or whisk them in a jug, then strain and serve. The cardamom makes a nice addition, taking this drink more in the direction of India than America.

ENOUGH FOR 8–10 MILKSHAKES

VARIATION – RASPBERRY YOGURT SHAKE:

This is also good made with fresh or frozen raspberries, but strain the purée to get rid of the pips.

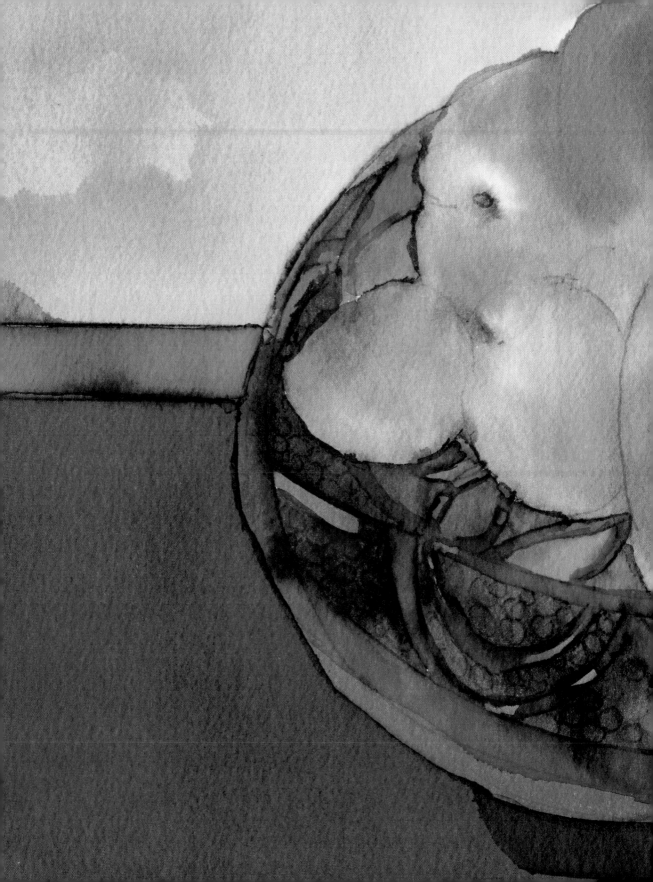

Maple pecan granola

A very tasty breakfast cereal, this, and rather more generous with the fruit and nuts than most commercial preparations. I devised it in response to the dearth of interesting ready-made organic breakfast cereals in the shops and continue to make it because we prefer it to the alternatives. Peanut (sometimes sold as groundnut) oil is recommended for its neutrality, but any light flavourless oil could be used. The soft, dried bananas can usually be tracked down in health food shops, if not in supermarkets.

- 60 ml peanut oil
- 120 ml maple syrup
- 500 g jumbo rolled oats

- 120 g pecan nuts, coarsely chopped
- 120 g dried bananas, sliced (the soft type, not banana chips)

Oven temperature: 160°C (325°F, gas 3) – adjust for fan ovens

You need a large roasting tin for this, about 40 cm × 28 cm or equivalent. If you use something smaller and deeper the timings will be way out.

1   Mix the oil and maple syrup in with the rolled oats. Spread the granola in a wide shallow tray and bake for a total of 1 hour in a pre-heated oven. Stir after the first 15 minutes, mixing in the sides to the middle, thereafter stir every 10 minutes, until oats are evenly golden brown and crisp. After 45 minutes add the pecan nuts.

2   Stir in the sliced bananas (separate them with your fingers if necessary) and allow the granola to cool completely before storing in an airtight container.

Roast pepper sandwich with pesto and Parmesan

This is more a suggestion than a recipe as such, and makes for a succulent and tasty snack. If you're roasting vegetables for something else, it's always a good idea to bung in a few extra peppers as they are such a useful and delicious item to have around. I like to barbecue them over charcoal, weather permitting. If you don't have your own favourite method of roasting peppers you could follow or adapt the instructions in *Roast pepper and red onion salad with preserved lemon* (page 34).

- focaccia, split lengthwise, or some other good bread
- pesto (shop-bought is OK)
- roasted red and yellow peppers
- fresh basil leaves
- thin slivers of fresh Parmesan cheese
- sun-dried tomato paste
- salt and pepper

Spread one half of the focaccia with pesto, the other with sun-dried tomato paste. Arrange the peppers generously on one half of the bread, then add a few basil leaves and slivers or shavings of fresh Parmesan. Season with salt and pepper and put the two halves together.

Torta basilico

This is a very over-the-top creamy cheese and pesto savoury layer cake. Inspired by a gorgeous Italian cheese I used to buy at the Munich *Viktualienmarkt*, it's so rich you can almost feel your arteries hardening as you eat it, but for a special occasion it is festive, beautiful and delicious.

Give yourself plenty of time (about an hour) to make this. The assembly is quite time-consuming although not difficult. It's actually better made a day in advance, giving all the flavours time to mingle, but leave the garnish until the last minute. If the assembly procedure described below makes you nervous, build up the layers in a deep glass bowl so the stripes are visible through the sides.

- 250 g dolcelatte or Gorgonzola cheese, rind removed
- 250 g Mascarpone cheese
- salt to taste
- finely grated zest from 2 lemons
- 30 g basil leaves
- 2 cloves of garlic, crushed
- 40 g fresh Parmesan cheese, grated
- 2 tablespoons olive oil
- 100 g pine kernels

1 Beat both cheeses together until smooth, using an electric mixer, then add about a level teaspoon of salt and the grated lemon zest. Taste and add more salt if necessary.

2 To make the pesto, wash the basil leaves, drain and gently pat them dry with kitchen paper. Set aside a couple of perfect leaves for the garnish, then put the basil, garlic, Parmesan, olive oil, a pinch of salt and 70 g of the pine kernels into a food processor and whiz until smooth, stopping the machine and scraping the mixture down from the sides as necessary.

3 Now build up the layers. Pile the cheese mixture into a strong plastic food bag (you might need to put one bag inside another for reinforcement) and, with some sharp scissors, snip off a very small section of one corner to make a hole about 3 mm in diameter. Of course if you happen to own one you could use a piping bag and medium nozzle. Pipe the cheese in a circle, about 20 cm in diameter, directly onto the serving plate. Start from the outside of the circle and work inwards, filling in the gaps as you go. Use a knife to level the surface and patch any small holes.

4 Spoon some of the pesto onto the cheese layer and gently spread it over the surface of the cheese. Scatter the pesto with some of the remaining 30 g pine nuts. Pipe another layer of cheese on top of the pesto layer, making it very slightly smaller than the layer below. Now add another layer of pesto and more pine nuts, followed by another layer of cheese, and so on, finishing with a layer of cheese. For the sake of stability you should be aiming for a slightly domed effect, but don't worry if it looks a bit wonky – that's part of its charm. Just before serving garnish with a few extra pine nuts and a couple of fresh basil leaves.

SAUCES, CONDIMENTS AND SALAD DRESSINGS

Grilled red pepper and tomato sauce

A nice, simple sauce for pasta or baked potatoes. The tomatoes and onions are puréed from raw, which significantly reduces the cooking time needed and makes for a very fresh flavour.

- 1 red pepper, de-seeded and de-veined
- 1 tablespoon olive oil
- 3 ripe tomatoes, peeled
- 1 small onion, peeled and coarsely chopped
- 2 cloves of garlic, peeled and chopped
- ½ teaspoon salt

- 15 g butter
- 3 or 4 tablespoons double cream
- a few drops of Champagne vinegar
- salt and freshly ground black pepper
- 6 fresh basil leaves, chopped
- fresh grated Parmesan cheese to serve

Pre-heat your grill for a few minutes.

1   Cut the red pepper into chunky strips lengthwise, brush with olive oil and grill until tender, turning a few times. This takes about 20 minutes. The peppers shouldn't be too close to the heating element or they will burn before they are cooked through. When the peppers are cooked, cut them into small chunks.

2   Put the tomatoes, onion, garlic and salt in a food processor and whiz until smooth, scraping the bits down from the sides as necessary.

3   Heat the butter in a saucepan, add the tomato purée and cook gently for about 10 minutes, stirring occasionally. Stir in the cooked peppers and the cream and add a little Champagne vinegar to brighten the flavour. Check the seasoning and add more salt and pepper if necessary.

4   At the very last moment before serving stir in the shredded basil leaves. Serve on pasta or baked potatoes, with freshly grated Parmesan to pass round.

SERVES 2

Walnut sauce

This sauce is versatile and very simple to make. An unusual and delicious emollient for pasta, it takes most of its flavour from roasted walnuts. Don't be tempted to skip the roasting stage, or you are likely to be disappointed. The age of the nuts is also a critical factor – the fresher the better. The sauce also makes a good accompaniment for asparagus or raw vegetables and, as if that were not enough, when cold it sets and makes a delicious, light spread for bread or crackers.

To roast the nuts, put them on a baking sheet in a pre-heated oven at 180°C (350°F, gas 4) for 9–12 minutes. Adjust the temperature for fan ovens. Watch them like a hawk – they tend to burn very suddenly. The nuts should be a warm brown colour all the way through – break one in half to check.

- 120 g roasted walnut pieces
- 1 clove garlic, peeled and crushed
- $\frac{1}{2}$–$\frac{3}{4}$ teaspoon salt
- 3 tablespoons walnut oil
- $1\frac{1}{2}$ level teaspoons caster sugar
- 4 tablespoons cream
- grated nutmeg to taste
- 3–4 tablespoons boiling water
- fresh grated Parmesan cheese, if serving with pasta

1 Tip the roasted nuts into a colander and shake well to remove as much of the loose skin as possible. The more you manage to lose, the less likely it is that the sauce will be bitter, as can occasionally happen. A thorough roasting of the nuts is also helpful in this regard (see above).

2 Put all the ingredients except the water and Parmesan in a food processor and whiz, stopping the motor and scraping the mixture down from the sides as necessary. Trickle the hot water through the food processor spout with the machine running, until the sauce is smooth and pale with a creamy consistency. Taste and adjust the seasoning.

3 Serve the sauce stirred into cooked hot pasta and top with plenty of fresh grated Parmesan cheese.

ENOUGH FOR 3 ON PASTA

VARIATION – PASTA WITH ROCKET AND WALNUT SAUCE
Coarsely chop 100 g of fresh rocket and stir into the hot pasta until wilted, before adding the walnut sauce. Serve with fresh grated Parmesan cheese.

Blue cheese dressing

Seriously out of fashion at the moment, blue cheese dressing is nevertheless one of the most delicious concoctions there is! I therefore make no apologies for including this recipe here. A lovely way of jazzing up a chunky but plain iceberg and watercress salad, it also makes a good addition to sandwiches, baked potatoes, chips, etc. During times of stress I've been known to sneak downstairs at midnight and eat it straight from the jar on a finger. . .

The amount of cheese you use depends on its strength of flavour. Roquefort is more intense than Gorgonzola, so you will need less. Let your taste buds decide.

- 60–90 g Gorgonzola, Roquefort or other exceptionally delicious blue cheese (see above)
- 4 tablespoons olive oil
- juice of about half a lemon
- 1–2 tablespoons Champagne vinegar or other mild white wine vinegar
- salt and pepper
- small splash of boiling water to thin (optional)

1 Put the cheese, olive oil, half the lemon juice and 1 tablespoon of vinegar in the food processor and whiz until smooth. Taste, add salt and pepper as necessary, then add more lemon juice if you think it needs sharpening up a little. You may want to add more Champagne vinegar too – it just depends on the cheese. The dressing is likely to be quite solid so thin it with a little hot water if you want it more runny.

2 If you refrigerate the dressing for any length of time before use it will probably set even if you've already added some water – olive oil solidifies when very cold – so bring it to room temperature before deciding how much dilution is required. It keeps well in the fridge for several days.

Moroccan preserved lemons

This recipe is an adaptation of one I came across in Paula Wolfert's excellent book *Mediterranean Grains and Greens*, published by Kyle Cathie, 1999. Thanks to the publishers for permitting me to use it here.

Preserved lemons can be used to add their distinctive flavour to many different savoury dishes, but be warned – they are very addictive. For a while I was adding them to just about everything I cooked. Generally, you chop a chunk or two very finely and add it to whatever you're cooking near the start of the cooking time. It is sometimes recommended that you scrape off and discard the flesh, using only the rind, but I have not found this to be necessary – I use the whole lot, and often include some of the preserving liquid for good measure. When you've finished the lemons, the lemony oil makes a fantastic cooking medium, too.

- **4 or 5 ripe lemons**
- **75 g coarse sea salt**
- **olive oil**

1. Scrub and dry two of the lemons and cut them into chunks. I usually cut them into eighths, as this gives pieces of a useful size. Pack the chunks into a glass jar to which there is a non-reactive lid (i.e. one made from glass, cork, plastic or plastic-coated metal).

2. Squeeze the juice from the remaining lemons until you have 100 ml. Add the salt and lemon juice to the jar and keep it at room temperature with the lid on for 7 days. Shake the jar once a day during this time.

3. The lemons are now ready for use and will keep for a long time if covered with olive oil and stored in the fridge.

Green tomatillo salsa with lime and coriander

This fresh-tasting salsa is ideal as a starter for a Mexican meal, or as a dip with drinks. It also makes a good filling for ripe avocados. You may be lucky enough to find fresh tomatillos in ethnic food shops or supermarkets. When peeled, they look like small green (or occasionally purple) tomatoes, but as they are surrounded by a papery husk you wouldn't necessarily know. They have a crisp, refreshing texture, and taste something like apples. Despite superficial similarities in the name, they are not of the tomato family and are actually related to the little orange edible physalis (sometimes called Chinese gooseberry), which is now a common sight on exotic fruit stalls.

For the enterprising gardener they are no more difficult to grow than tomatoes and require similar treatment. In the UK I have ripened them outdoors in large plant pots placed against a south-facing wall. They have a strange, branching growth habit, needing both restraint (prune off some of the laterals) and support – the fruit gets too heavy for the stems. The plants benefit from a high-potash feeding regime. Try to water just enough to prevent the plants from wilting, as over-watering can cause them to split. They are ready to pick when the husks feel full and firm.

- 400 g fresh tomatillos
- ½ small red onion, finely chopped
- 1 fresh green or red chilli (more if you like), peeled, de-seeded and finely chopped
- 1 clove of garlic, crushed or finely chopped
- a generous handful of fresh coriander leaves
- 1 level teaspoon of salt
- about a tablespoon of olive oil
- fresh lime juice to taste – 1 lime should be more than enough
- tortilla chips or raw vegetables for dipping

1   Remove the papery husks from the tomatillos. They will feel very sticky underneath, so rinse and dry them. Chop them roughly, then put them in a food processor along with the red onion, chilli, garlic, coriander, salt and olive oil. It's definitely worth chopping the onion, chilli and garlic first to avoid unexpected lumps of anything too intense in the finished dish.

2   Whiz briefly to make a salsa that still retains some texture, then add fresh lime juice to taste and extra salt if necessary. Stir immediately before serving, as the salsa separates readily. The salsa is quite watery so serve it in individual portions, with a big bowl of tortilla chips or raw vegetables for dipping.

SERVES 4, AS A DIP WITH TORTILLA CHIPS

Smoked garlic and saffron mayonnaise

A delicious and pungent mayonnaise, this makes a lively addition to sandwiches, a good dip for crudités and is also quite at home stirred into a soup such as *Tomato and chickpea soup with saffron* (page 26).

- a pinch of saffron threads
- 3 or 4 cloves smoked garlic, peeled and crushed
- ¾ level teaspoon salt
- 1½ level teaspoons Dijon mustard
- 1 tablespoon white wine vinegar
- 1 tablespoon lemon juice
- 1 large egg
- 50 ml olive oil
- 200 ml groundnut oil or other very lightly flavoured salad oil

1 Put 1 tablespoon of boiling water in a cup, add the saffron threads, swirl to wet them and leave aside to soak for 15–20 minutes.

2 Place the garlic, salt, mustard, vinegar, lemon juice and egg in a blender or food processor and whiz briefly, then leave the motor running and start adding the oils, a drop at a time initially. Gradually increase the flow to a thin but steady stream, continuing until both the olive oil and groundnut oil have been incorporated.

3 When the saffron has soaked for at least 15 minutes, add it, complete with its soaking water, to the mayonnaise and whiz again briefly. Taste and adjust the seasoning if necessary. Store in the fridge in an airtight container and use within a week.

Roasted pepper vinaigrette

Make this lovely salad dressing when you've been roasting (or barbecuing) vegetables and have some cooked red pepper to spare. A method of roasting peppers is given on page 34.

For a really quick and hassle-free starter, fan out slices of ripe avocado on a plate, drizzle some of this over, scatter on a few roasted walnut pieces and serve with fingers of toast. The dressing is also good on a pasta salad, with appropriate vegetable additions. If you plan to use it this way be sure to pour it on while the pasta is still hot from the pan – you'll get a better flavour.

- 1 roasted red pepper
- 1 clove garlic, peeled and crushed
- 4 tablespoons olive oil
- 2 tablespoons Champagne vinegar
- 1 teaspoon balsamic vinegar
- salt and pepper

Coarsely chop the red pepper and put it and the garlic in a food processor. With the machine running, pour the oil and vinegars in a steady stream through the spout until you have a smooth purée. You may need to stop the machine once or twice and scrape the mixture down from the sides. Season the dressing to taste with salt and pepper.

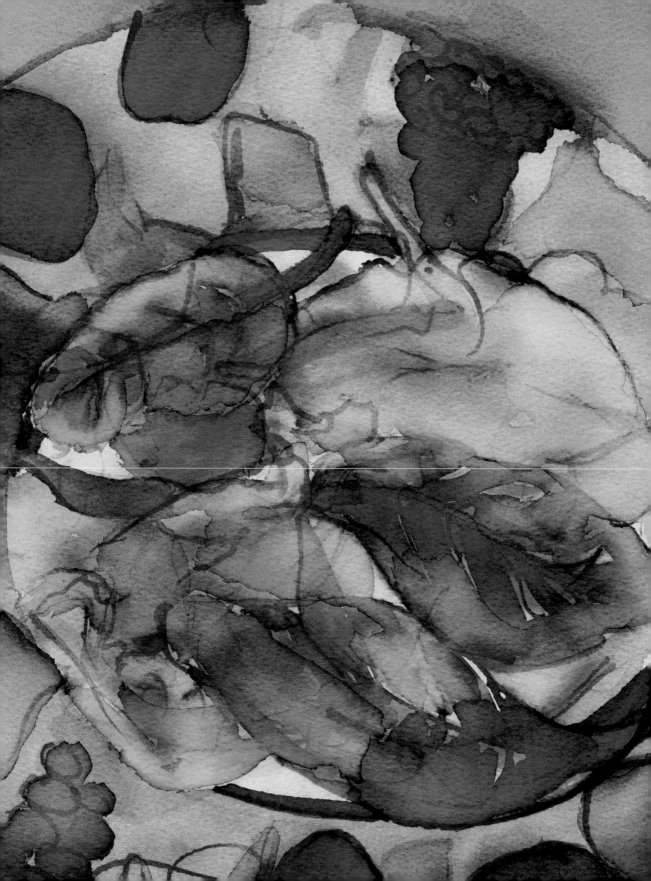

INDEX

Wild mushroom and potato gratin with lemon salsa verde, 62

Wolfert, Paula, 198

Y

yogurt
    Banana yogurt ice, 161
    Blackberry yogurt ice, 150
    Damson yogurt ice, 155
    Strawberry yogurt shake, 185

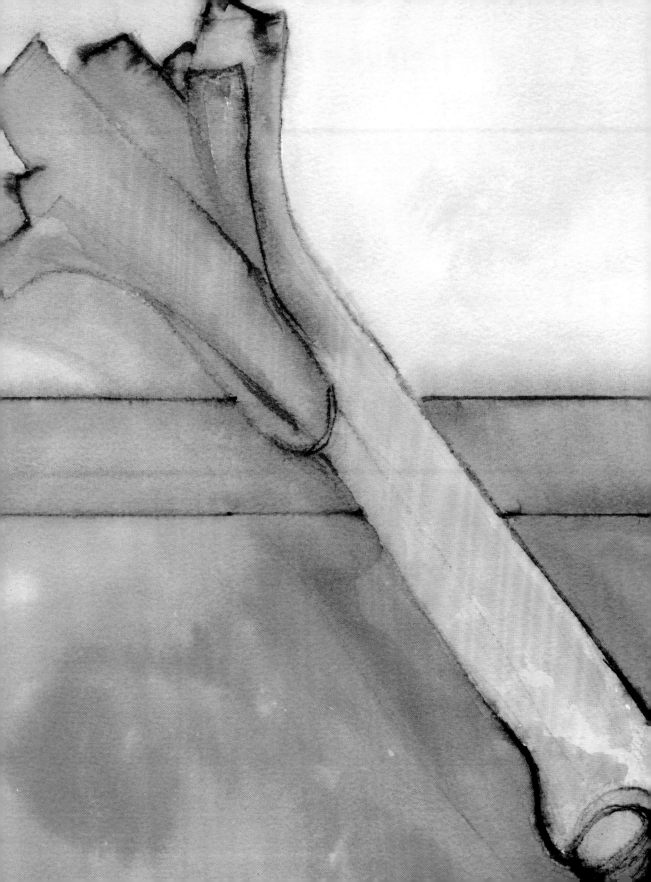

LIST OF ILLUSTRATIONS

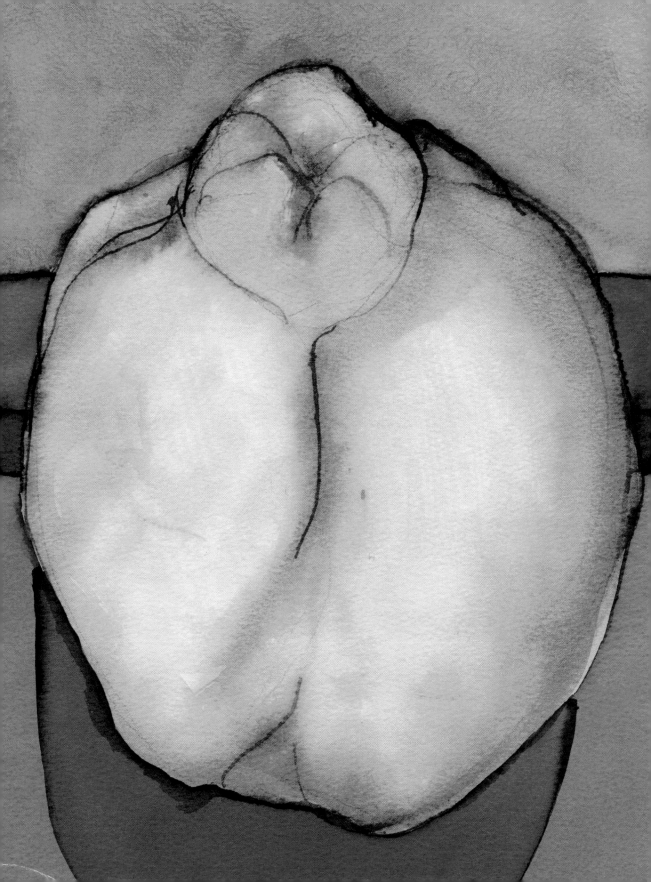

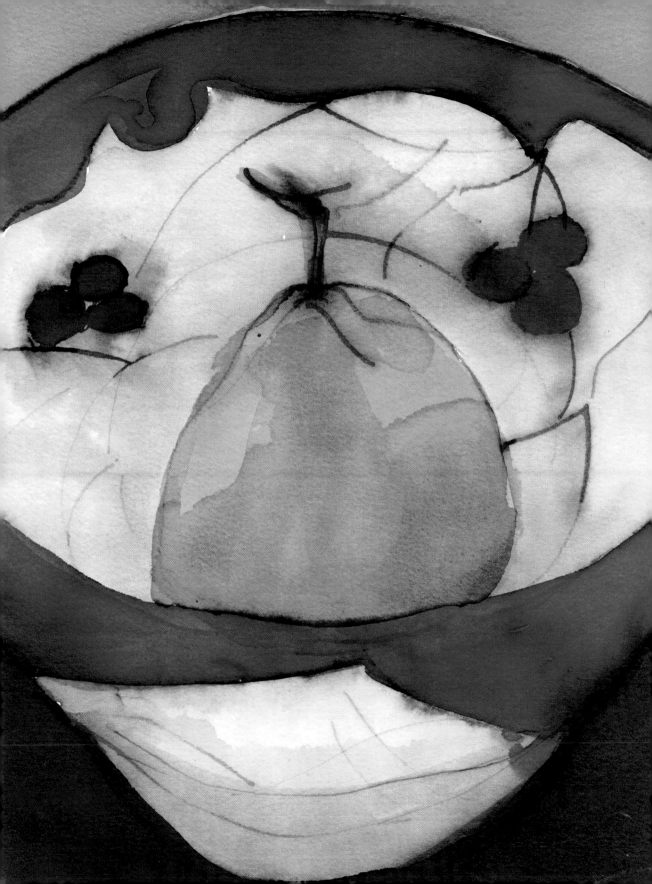

VEGETABLE HEAVEN PRINTS

Damsons

Plum

Lemons

Oranges

Pumpkins and Chillies

Red Pepper

Two Figs on a Blue Plate

Quinces

Pot of Basil

Tomatoes

Swede

Fennel on a Yellow Plate

These open edition giclée prints on fine quality watercolour paper are sized to fit standard frames. The giclée printing process uses an extended ink set to give optimal colour reproduction which brings out the full vibrancy of the original paintings.

	Approximate Image size	Paper/frame size	Price
Small	25 × 35 cm	40 × 50 cm	£20
Medium	36 × 50 cm	50 × 70 cm	£30
Large	46 × 63 cm	60 × 80 cm	£40

UK mainland carriage for up to twelve prints is £3

Order on-line from **www.pauntley-prints.co.uk/vh** or phone **01531 829902**

All major credit and debit cards accepted

FULL MONEY-BACK GUARANTEE